Coaltown Revisited:
An Appalachian Notebook

Coaltown Revisited

An Appalachian Notebook

by Bill Peterson

Henry Regnery Company • Chicago

Cover photo and photo insert by John Fetterman.

To Linda and Chad,
that they may know
and understand
the people of coaltown

Contents

Acknowledgments

Dozens of people helped me with this book. Most of them live in quaint-sounding places like Eureka Hollow, Granny's Branch, Hot Spot, Bright Shade and Poor Bottom. They are kind, generous people, proud to be called hillbillies. I wish to thank all of them for sharing their front porches, fireplaces and days with a curious stranger. I am also deeply indebted to John Fetterman for talking me into it; Ward Sinclair, for his insight and UMW files; my bosses at the *Louisville Courier-Journal* for their encouragement; Joseph "Chip" Yablonski, Jr., Mike Trbovitch, Harry M. Caudill, Dr. and Mrs. Donald Rasmussen and Dan Gibson for being reminders that there are good people not afraid to stick out their necks; and Linda, a good editor and wife.

Coaltown Revisited:
An Appalachian Notebook

Introduction

They came, that wet, surprisingly cool spring of 1960, streaming into southwestern West Virginia. Past the slag heaps, the rusted auto carcasses and "blowed out" mines and into the hollows and coalcamps with the quaint-sounding names—Cabin Creek, Crab Orchard, Slab Fork and Pocahontas. The candidate with his Palm Beach tan, his two brothers, the pollsters and an ever-growing army of newsmen and photographers to woo, to gawk, to prod and to promise.

In one of those quirks that make American politics so unpredictable, the nation's eyes were focused for a brief moment on the West Virginia primary election, which pitted John F. Kennedy, then 42 and a U.S. Senator from Massachusetts, against Hubert H. Humphrey of Minnesota. Each sought to become the Democratic candidate for President of the United States. The primary was crucial for Kennedy. In it he had to prove that a Catholic could win in an almost totally Protestant area, supposedly rank with religious bigotry. The southwestern part of the state was particularly important. A Louis Harris poll had found the area to have the highest amount of anti-Catholic sentiment in the state. Even more significantly, the region, then as now, was ruled by powerful political barons who regularly deliver impressive majorities to candidates able to curry their favor and fill their campaign chests.

West Virginia was one of the nation's most depressed areas, a pocket of poverty in history's richest land. Automation had displaced 77,000 coal miners in the state during the 1950's. Unemployment exceeded 30 percent in some counties. The state's youth were fleeing, and more than half of its 164,000 aged earned annual incomes below $1,500.

With Franklin Delano Roosevelt, Jr.—whose late father is still looked on as a god in the area—at his side, Kennedy hopped from hamlet to hamlet. He spoke on the steps of a dozen decaying courthouses, and when his voice became so hoarse that he could speak no more, his brother Ted took over. John Kennedy saw the straggling lines of unemployed on the roadsides, the hundreds of families subsisting on welfare checks. Coal dust collected on his mop of chestnut hair and his blue tailored suit as he shook hands with miners at places like Itmann and Sophia.

The Harvard-educated son of a multimillionaire was shocked by what he saw. His aide and biographer, Theodore Sorenson, later wrote: "He more deeply understood, as the distressed areas of Massachusetts had never made him understand, the unemployed worker, the pensioner, the relief recipient and the ghost town and he more fervently endorsed their pleas for more help."

Kennedy's message that spring was chilling; his solutions, warmed-over New Deal. In county seat after county seat, his promise was the same: that whether he was in the White House or the Senate "the problems of this state will be on the desk of the next President." He talked of new highways, shifting defense spending, luring new industry and revamping the federal government's surplus-food distribution system.

And so the candidate came down state highway 16 out of Mullens and into Pineville, past Wolf Pen and into Welch, called "the nation's coal bin" by the local chamber of commerce. Mrs. Dandalo Agostine and a band of her neighbors flagged him down in front of the cinder-block house her husband built on the edge of town. Mrs. Agostine gave the candidate a drink of homebrew beer from a brown mug, which she persuaded his brother, Robert, to drink out of eight years later when he made the same trip. The candidate embraced her and chatted in Italian with her husband. Then he was off to the municipal parking lot where, coal dust still on his face, he said: "Unless the next administration deals with the question of what to do with men when machines have thrown them out of work . . . what has happened here in West Virginia is going to happen all across the country."

Welch . . . Superior . . . Big Four . . . Kimball . . . Vivian . . . Poor Bottom . . . Landgraff . . . Eckman . . . Keystone . . . the caravan moved from the narrow valley of the Tug River out onto U.S. 52 toward the Blue Ridge Mountains of Virginia. This was coal country deep in recession, a tough land where a man might work all week in a coal mine for $20 and feel lucky to get it. One man in five couldn't find a job. Each town had the look of the one before it. Once-prosperous Main Streets were pockmarked with empty storefronts.

The pitch was down home: meet the local folks, hint about the candidate's war record, promise jobs and win the political pros. McDowell County bought it. Kennedy forged an alliance with the powerful, but conservative, Christie Machine that had controlled county politics for two decades. (Sidney L. Christie was later appointed to a U.S. district court judgeship, a $40,000-a-year-for-life post, for his efforts.)

"Kennedy kidded with me. He was a real nice fellow," recalls Mike Gianoto, owner of Gianoto Grocery, who still keeps a picture *Life* magazine took of Kennedy holding his son, Mike, Jr. "I'd still vote for any Kennedy."

Kennedy won the West Virginia primary with the help of a 11,626-vote margin in McDowell County and clearly established himself as the frontrunner for the Democratic nomination. But, according to those closest to him, he never forgot what he had encountered in the coalcamps of West Virginia. One of his first acts after election as President was to create a special "depressed area commission" headed by former U.S. Senator Paul Douglas. The commission and the modest—by today's standards—proposals it advocated foreshadowed a decade-long obsession with the problems of the poor. First came the speeches, the countless magazine articles and a trickle of federal dollars for food-stamp programs and area redevelopment. "The Great Society," "The War on Poverty," the federal millions and a new generation of "do-gooders" followed in the Johnson administration. Their vision was a grand one. Dole would be dead. The poor—particularly the blacks in the ghettos and the whites in the hollows of Appalachia—would be saved. The American Dream would work for the disadvantaged.

Now, 12 years have passed since John Kennedy discovered poverty in West Virginia, and a new presidential campaign is upon us. The creekbeds have been discovered, agonized over and forgotten. The poor, who were suddenly important, are still there. Life in coaltown is much the same as Kennedy and those who followed him in 1960 saw it.

Part 1

Of Hope and Dismay

1

Coaltown Revisited

Coaltowns, like T-shirts, come in three basic sizes—small, medium and large. Welch, the county seat and home of the area's only Sears, Roebuck outlet, is McDowell County's one large coaltown. A half-dozen smaller places are medium-sized coaltowns, ranging from War, with a population of 3,006, to Keystone, once the home of southern West Virginia's best-known whorehouse district, Cinder Bottom. Eureka Hollow is the smallest of the small coaltowns. It doesn't have a single school, or grocery store, or gas station, or tavern. In fact, about all it has is a road paved with red dog [a rusty red residue from burning slag heaps], 2 rows of houses at the bottom of a fold in a mountain, 2 churches, 30 ponies, 25 cows, 75 families and 1 industry—poverty.

It was a sultry afternoon in late July when I first visited the hollow. The air was still, and dust from the road hung in

3

heavy clouds. I parked my car on the edge of one cloud and headed toward a weatherbeaten frame house. A short, bronzed man with deep lines around his eyes and tattered tennis shoes on his feet swayed back and forth on a porch swing. My task was uncertain. In 1960 John F. Kennedy had driven past the mouth of the hollow on U.S. 52. He hadn't stopped, but he had made promises up and down the roadway.

Earl Bowman, the man with the worn tennis shoes, turned out to be a Democratic precinct captain. Of course he remembered Kennedy's visits. JFK, he recalled, had stopped down the road at Keystone.

"He had the poor man on his mind—Roosevelt was the same way," said Bowman. "Everyone figured he'd do this country some good."

Had he? Had anyone? Had anything changed since Kennedy visited the county almost three elections ago?

Earl Bowman shrugged his shoulders. "The way I see it," he said, "this country's 'bout gone."

His neighbor, Mrs. Sarah "Granny" McPeak, agreed. She and her husband first moved to the hollow 40 years ago. In those days there were jobs for anyone who wanted work and the Eureka Coal Company kept the homes it rented to its employees painted and in good repair. The coal company sold out years ago. Today another company, Pocahontas Fuel, owns the houses. Paint has peeled off most of them. Porches sag and rusty tin cans and broken Big Red soda bottles litter the shallow creek that slithers down the hollow.

"Now I don't have no education," Granny said as she stirred a pot of homegrown green beans that night, "but it's my belief that things just got worser. A lot of folks here would still like to help themselves. But there's nothing around for them to try to better themselves."

She wiped her hands on a soiled apron and crossed the

room to a tiny window. "Each year life gets harder and harder here," she said. "People on high incomes, their wages keep going up. But you take us on low incomes, our income stays the same and our prices keep going up just like those on high incomes. It looks unfair to me."

The War on Poverty with all its federal dollars and hopeful rhetoric reached Eureka Hollow in 1965, the same year Congress passed an allied but more business-oriented law, the Appalachian Regional Act. Actually, a few small-fry forerunners of the two programs had been around for almost four years, and McDowell County, because it played a crucial role in electing John Kennedy, had received more than its fair share of federal largess. It was the first county in the nation, for example, to test the federal food-stamp program established by Kennedy's first executive order the day after his inauguration. Unemployed fathers, dubbed "Kennedy Children" by local wags, were put to work—mostly clearing brush from roadsides—under retraining and public-works programs that same year.

The 1965 effort was different. It was a crusade, begun with the blessings of a new president, a man who had once been poor himself. Each county had to plan its own strategy and form new agencies to carry it out. McDowell County called its effort the Council of Southern Mountains, West Virginia Branch, McDowell County Chapter, Inc. (to distinguish it from an Appalachian-wide organization of the same name headquartered in Berea, Kentucky). Its battle plan covered 124 pages and called for $721,846, all but about $74,000 to be federal money, in ammunition.

Only a tiny portion of this sum ever reached Eureka Hollow. The council hired Mrs. Cecil Holland, a coal miner's wife, to work in the hollow and the adjoining community of Eckman. Her first order of business was to survey the area and tell the people about a new community center at the old schoolhouse in Vivian, four miles away. The results of the survey weren't surprising. It showed that three-fourths of the families had incomes below the federal poverty level of $3,000 a year; that most lived in substandard housing; that educational levels were low (21.3 percent of the county's population is functionally illiterate, compared with a national average of 7.8 percent); that women headed one-fifth of the families; that a disproportionate number of people were either too young or too old to work for a living.

The new community center, one of nine set up in the county, created some enthusiasm. Most families sent their children to the preschool Head Start classes it offered. Several women enrolled in sewing classes. Others encouraged their families to take advantage of the center's health services. Granny McPeak joined an adult-education course to work toward a high-school-equivalency diploma. Several men eventually found their way onto the rolls of one of a succession of job-training programs, which rarely offered any real training. Later a small community-action group started in the hollow. It talked of cleanup campaigns and of building a community water system—a dream never realized. And in the summer of 1969, its members helped vacationing students from William and Mary College build the hollow's first playground.

But always there were obstacles, many too powerful to overcome. One was the people themselves. Some were too proud to ask for help, or "mess with that poverty business." Others were too emotionally or physically defeated by life in coaltown to do much about it. Still others appeared to be, as Michael Harrington suggested in his book *The Other America,* immune to progress. They simply were not interested in helping themselves, or were incapable of doing so.

The poor received little understanding from county officials. Some resisted antipoverty programs from the start. Others resented any implication that their county was poor. A few were, as one observer suggested, "so conservative that they made Calvin Coolidge look like a left winger." Tom Sinclair was one of them.

Tom Sinclair

Sinclair has strong opinions about the federal government, poor people, welfare and McDowell County. He has had experience with all four. He served 24 years as an elected county official, his last in 1970 as president of the county court, the county's highest executive body.

"I don't like the federal government, period," he said in his office in the aging McDowell County Courthouse, which overlooks Welch. "I don't even like buying a postage stamp from the federal government.

"It appears that all anyone in the federal government thinks you have to do is just hold out a bunch of money and they can cure all your ills.

"Anyone who really wants a job can get one here," he continued. "These people with their federal programs could get out and we wouldn't see the difference. Welfare was here before they came and it will be here after they leave."

Sinclair's low opinion of the federal government was reinforced when he passed DuPont Circle on his way to the Appalachian Regional Commission's office in Washington. "The place was full of those dirty, long-haired hippies. You've never seen anything like it," he said. "There were a lot of people there that we'd run out of McDowell County."

Sinclair was 70 years old when he made that visit. A few months later his career of "public service" was brought to a halt in a Democratic primary election. Before he left office, he told me that McDowell County's biggest problem for the 1970's is people who don't want to work. "Welfare is giving away money like it's going out of style," he said. "It's gotten so if you want to go out and hire someone you can't find anyone because they can make more money on welfare."

The U.S. Office of Economic Opportunity (OEO), the national antipoverty agency, did little to quell the suspicions of mountain politicians like Tom Sinclair. Its priorities vacillated continuously, its understanding of and methods of attack on Appalachian problems even more so. Everything it did was on a crash basis. The money was there. It had to be spent immediately. In theory, the poor were to have a say in how it was spent. In practice, the purse strings were controlled by Washington. "It seemed that the programs that were most beneficial to the poor got cut out each year," complained Harold Cooper, a former schoolteacher who became executive director of the Council of Southern Mountains. "They'd sit in an office in Washington and write something that looked beautiful on paper, but it wasn't worth a damn here."

This process reached ridiculous extremes. On one occasion, Cooper asked a new OEO field representative for money to transport the poor to council functions. The OEO rep, a young girl with a degree from a prestigious Eastern university, replied quite earnestly: "Tell you what I'll do. I'll put $2,000 in your budget for subway tokens."

The results were predictable. "I'd say they're about nil," said Roland L. Taylor, editor and publisher of the *Welch Daily News*. "We've spent millions of dollars and I can't tell you a single solitary thing that has been accomplished. We've paid a lot of staff people, local people, to accomplish very little. We've been surveyed and analyzed by every department of government. Everyone in town is just sick and tired of it."

Neither the OEO nor the Appalachian Regional Commission nor anyone else left much that was permanent in McDowell County. After a dozen years of "economic development" the county has 3,000 fewer jobs than it did in 1960. Only one new industry—a small sewing factory, which employs only women—has opened, and its future is dim. There are no new roads. Even short stretches of four-lane highway are unheard of. The nearest interstate highway is 45 miles from Welch. New housing is scarce, and much of the county lacks an adequate water supply. Until these problems are resolved, industrial development remains the pipedream it was when John F. Kennedy first visited the county in 1960.

In the meantime, the county continues to export its two most valuable resources—its coal and its people. During the 1960's, 28 percent of the population left because there were no jobs. About 95 percent of the graduates of the county's fine vocational school joined the exodus. At the same time the riches from the county's coal flowed into corporate coffers in Pittsburgh and New York. Coal's absentee ownership continues to be a giant stumbling block to progress. Nine coal and landholding companies own or control 80 percent of the land in the county. Eight of them are "outsiders" with little concern for the welfare of the poor. One of them, the Pocahontas Land Corporation, a subsidiary of the Norfolk and Western Railway, singlehandedly controls an estimated 35 percent of the county's land.

Little of this, the oppression of poverty and hopelessness, is obvious in Welch, the county seat. There coal is still king, and the coal business is booming. Rail cars piled high with the rich black rock rumble through town from the big deep mines owned by the U.S. Steel, Consolidation and Island Creek Coal companies, bound for steel furnaces in Gary, Pittsburgh and Japan. Pocahontas Fuel, nicknamed "Pokee Fuel," has opened up a new mine in nearby Maitland. Mines are hiring young, inexperienced miners for the first time in a generation. Unemployment is down to just over 8 percent, compared with 23.5 percent in 1960, only 3 points above the national average. Crude chalkmarks on a blackboard in the window of the state employment office advertise: "Wanted: Augermen, Pumpman, End Loader Operator, Bulldozerman, Driller, Meat Cutter, Mine Electrician (must be in good health willing to work underground)." "Anyone who isn't too sorry to work can get a job," one old hand advises.

The boom shows up in the storefronts and on the streets. Young blacks (the county has one of the largest black populations in Appalachia) with Afros and bellbottom trousers stroll the sidewalks and get into late-model Buicks and Oldsmobiles with "Bluefield State" and "Howard University" decals on the back windows. The assets of the McDowell County National Bank are up to more than $28 million. City Mayor W. B. Swope, a one-eyed Republican, flies his own private plane. "I don't think we're so poor here," he says.

But there is a different, more representative face of Appalachia during the 1970's. It's found in the small coaltowns like Eureka Hollow. Life there is as different from that in Welch as life on the near West Side of Chicago is from that in the silk-stocking suburbs of Kenilworth and Winnetka. Ask a county-seat businessman about Eureka Hollow, for instance, and he'll tell you it has a tough reputation. It's a hard place to collect bills, he'll say, the home of "do-less" people, "too sorry to work, always looking for something for nothing."

The people of coaltown resent this reputation. It's unfair and misleading, they say. It doesn't consider that the hollow, like anyplace else, has its own social order, its devout mothers and hardworking fathers along with its loose women and drunkards, its oasis of prosperity (working coal miners make upwards of $35 a day) along with its slums. They would like the businessmen—or any others—who condemn them to come to Eureka Hollow one day and try to get to know them and the way they live. The old people, of whom there are many, are the most profitable to visit. They sit on their porches or in front of their fireplaces: the women with the special serenity that comes from raising a brood of children and doing it well; the men with their tattered bodies and their memories of the mines. There are many such men.

Claude Bowman

Slowly, painfully, Claude Bowman clenched and unclenched his left fist, staring at its white scar tissue.

"It won't go right. I do this every day and it doesn't get any better," he said. "I can't even get a job—you know they aren't going to hire anyone with hands like this."

Claude Bowman's hand, his face and about three-fourths of his body were burned in a mine explosion. It happened about 3:00 A.M. He and his partner were alone in a mine, making a safety inspection.

"The first thing I knowed there was a spark," he said. "The next thing I was hollering for help. I don't know how long I'd been out. My partner, he was blowed back two breakrows (about 120 feet) around a corner."

The two men dragged their torn bodies 3,000 feet to safety. Bowman was hospitalized for two months. Now he spends his days on the front porch of his small, gray-shingled house, clenching and unclenching his fists. He is 53, thick-chested and hearty-looking. He'll probably never work again. His biggest hope is that he may be declared permanently disabled. But even this is in doubt. In the meantime, there is a terse bitterness in his voice when he says he didn't allow any of his sons to work in the mines.

"I knowed better than to raise 'em up for that," he said.

Mine accidents killed 942 men in West Virginia during the 1960's. The names of scores more who died slower deaths don't appear in the statistics. Claude Bowman's brother was one of them. The doctor said it was a heart attack, but his widow, Ruth Bowman, and everyone else on the hollow knows it was "dust on the lung"—also known as "black lung" or coal miner's pneumoconiosis, a chronic disease among coal miners.

Ruth Bowman still lives in the hollow about two city blocks from her brother-in-law. She looked very suburban in her striped pullover, scooped low at the neck, and blue shorts and sandals.

"This isn't a pretty place to look at, but there's a lot of love here . . . there's a welcome feeling," she said.

Her place is Eureka Hollow's soda fountain, record shop, teen club and YMCA all rolled into one. The kids—ranging in age from 3 to 20—come to buy candy or soda pop, to sit, to listen to records, to rap. They tell Mrs. Bowman their troubles, their heartaches. She knows who has a crush on whom, who is having a tough time in school or with his parents. Some stay all night. Many hang around every afternoon.

"I figure they all have a need," she said. "I'm a good listener. The children don't seem to get enough attention—love."

There was a sadness in her deep brown eyes as she spoke.

She has troubles of her own. Her husband worked 21 years in the mines but quit on doctor's orders 2 years before he died. This means that she doesn't qualify for a widow's pension from the United Mine Workers union (UMW), and because she isn't old enough and her own children left home long ago, she isn't eligible for any public-assistance program.

She sometimes worries about how to support herself. So far she has made do with part-time jobs with the Council of Southern Mountains. She tried to get a full-time job with the antipoverty agency, but nothing was available. Otherwise there just isn't much for a middle-aged woman to do in McDowell County.

But mostly Ruth Bowman worries about the children. Eureka Hollow has more of them than anything else. She counts 37 in 6 houses surrounding hers. The kids are all over the place. They're playing in the street. They're hanging on fences and porches. Many of them are dirty. Their families don't have running water for bathtubs. Some are clothed in rags. Ruth Bowman would like to help them.

"I'd like to do a lot of things—to give us a better way of life," she said remorsefully. "But I don't know how. And I can't do it alone. We need someone to help."

Life in the hollow is on the road. Sedans and pickups bounce by on their way to the Eckman post office in the old brick headquarters of the Pulaski Mine Company. Coal trucks pass carrying 30-ton loads. Swirling clouds of dust. Chickens, ducks, cows, ponies, kids, old men. And stares. Road watching is Eureka Hollow's number-one sport. It's done from porches and behind curtains. "Everyone wants to know what everyone else is doing," one woman explained. "And usually they do. By noontime, I can find out what almost everyone in the hollow had for breakfast."

Promises

William Dean, a veteran of 43 years in the mines, watched the road from his yard near the mouth of the hollow.

"Basically a whole lot of things Kennedy promised we haven't seen happen," he said. "I believe if he was around things would be different. With that man Kennedy, things opened up. Now they're sliding downhill.

"What impressed people here most was he came to meet the people—to see the conditions," he said. "That's the reason he went over so."

Today Dean's two biggest concerns are corruption in his union, the UMW, and the lack of "workin'" industries in the county.

"The union it's just like gangsters. It used to be they robbed a bank with a gun," Dean said. "Now they sit down and steal it with a pencil and paper. Tony Boyle [UMW president] won't come here. He's afraid 'cause everyone is so down on him. We'd run him out like we did our district UMW president the last time he came around. We ganged up on him and worked over his car."

Dean and many of his friends were intrigued with the possibility of new industry for the county in the early 1960's—a possibility some businessmen say was opposed by coal interests. Dean explained why.

"You think if I could get a factory job, I'd work in a coal mine? You know I wouldn't. You'd have to be crazy. Workin' industry, that was my big hope."

Without "workin' industries," the citizens of Eureka Hollow have only two sources to turn to for their livelihood—coal and government checks. Dean is in the minority. He still turns to coal. The majority turns to checks. They draw welfare checks or food stamps or Social Security checks or all three. The checks form the backbone of the hollow's economy and are always good for conversation. Those who get them justifiably feel they are never quite enough. Those who don't get checks feel they promote "sorriness" or at least a sort of con-artistry.

Robert Olah

Stoic and slowmoving after 42 years in the mines, Robert Olah was talking about checks on the front porch of his sister-in-law's house. He didn't believe in them. He said he applied for food stamps once, but was refused after he filled out several sheets of embarrassing questions (Do you own a home? Do you have a savings account? What payments are you making?). He was disgusted when it all went for naught. "I just gave them a good cussing and left," he said. "Won't try it again for nothing. 'Druther starve."

Just then Alfred Grim's pickup wheeled to a stop, and Robert Caudill, Olah's brother-in-law, got out. The two were among several thousand miners in West Virginia, and parts of Kentucky and Pennsylvania, out on strike. They both had been to the food-stamp office in Welch.

Caudill was perplexed because he had been refused stamps after he correctly stated his income for the month as $290. "I can't understand it," he said. "Some of them came out of there with a stack of food stamps. Guess I was the only one who told the truth. That's what I told them. I wouldn't lie."

Alfred Grim leaned out the pickup window. He had gotten some food stamps, but not nearly what he felt he deserved. "It gets you how some of them was lying," he said. "Men who are working right beside you, doing the same job, making the same money. That one dirty bastard got $165 worth of stamps for $40. Man, if I could talk like some people I never would have to work a lick."

Caudill threw down his black felt derby hat. He said he would go back another day.

Grim, still in the pickup, was in a jovial mood. "Tell you how to get 'em," he advised. "You put on some raggedy old clothes and get two crutches and go in there. Then you'll get 'em."

And Tomorrow

A petite brunette with flowing hair and a white lace dress, her bosoms pinched tight against her chest, clasped her hands together. "I beg your prayers for my two brothers up in Ohio so they may see the Lord," she cried.

The girl had a scrubbed, almost saintly look about her. It was hard to imagine what her brothers could be up to. But her request hit a responsive chord. Soon almost everyone on the two rows of benches in the Eckman Church of God was joining her, offering special requests of their own. Most were for kids, teen-agers especially, that they be saved. "Lord, watch over our young people," one elderly woman pleaded. A teen-ager asked for virtue so she could serve God. "Keep my sons from wandering, O God," said a mother behind her. "Don't let our children stray from the path so they tangle with the law," prayed another.

Eureka Hollow, like everyplace else, is worried about its kids. Its parents want their children to have a better life than their own. They're proud of them, they're concerned. They fret that some of them drink beer when they're too young, or get rowdy at one of the joints in a neighboring community, or that there isn't much for them to do around home. It bothers them that some don't have jobs, that others don't have parents who are interested in them, and that some may have to spend their lives underground in a coal mine.

The children are tomorrow. What will become of them? If the last generation is any indication, a few of those from the better families will go to work in the mines. The rest of the brighter ones will leave Eureka Hollow and probably West Virginia as well. They'll join the army, or take a factory job in some far-off place such as Virginia or North Carolina or Ohio. Some might even make it to Detroit or Chicago. Most will be poorly prepared for what they encounter.

Some who leave will return. Some of them will get jobs and become productive members of the community. A few others will join their parents and the young people who didn't have enough guts or ambition to leave in the first place on the porches and welfare rolls.

I asked Mickey Jackson, a high-school dropout, about a group of ten guys playing football on a bare spot of ground in Eureka Hollow's tiny playground.

"Oh, most eveybody will leave. Go to the service and such. But they'll come back. Won't work though."

Why?

" 'Cause we're too sorry," he said.

2

The Promised Land

In the lushness of summer it isn't hard to imagine what the land was like 200 years ago. The green leaves of the locust, the scrub oak and the poplar cover the scars. Their beauty lures, mesmerizes, overwhelms. The narrow blacktop highways add to the dizziness. For long moments the traveler feels he is riding an endless black snake slithering its way through a gigantic green carpet humped and creased into narrow valleys and jagged mountains. But just as the image firmly focuses itself, the blacktop snake rounds a bend and there is a stream choked with rusty tin cans, a hillside stripped bare by bulldozers or a sallow-cheeked child with a dirty face.

This is Daniel Boone country—Appalachia, the original American frontier, the land of the coonskin cap, where the fiercely independent woodsmen-pioneers fought the red man to open the trails westward. It is a land risen from the floor of an ancient inland sea, a strange, wonderful land with eight million inhabitants that extends from Pennsylvania to northern Alabama. In size and shape it roughly resembles California. Its great irony is that it contains some of the nation's richest resources and its poorest people.

In midwinter the poverty is easier to see. The hillsides are bleak and gray. The leaves have fallen and craggy-faced old men with gunny sacks slung over their shoulders walk the highways picking up chunks of coal that have fallen from passing trucks.

One January day I stopped to ask one of these men if he knew of a coal-buying cooperative that a local antipoverty group had started in a nearby county seat to provide cheap fuel for people like himself. The man, his chin buried deep in his coat collar, looked at me in disbelief.

"War on poverty, muleshit," he said as he spat into the dust. "That ain't ever did nothing for me."

He turned and continued on his way.

The encounter tells us something about the Appalachian mountaineer, his independence and his view of life. For this man and thousands like him, the entire history of the region is one of betrayed hopes and broken promises. They have watched the rest of the nation move ahead—often on their television screens—while they go on living in a depressed area, as depressed human beings. They have looked toward their institutions and leaders for help and have listened to their promises. But these same institutions, the nation's callousness and the region's geography have conspired to destroy their aspirations.

The first broken promise was the land itself. Two hundred years ago it was teeming with game and unspent resources—lofty sycamores and beeches, wild turkey and beaver, elk and buffalo, partridge and wildcat—a land so rugged and mysterious that even the Choctaw and the Shawnee visited its deepest bowels only on occasional hunting trips.

The first wave of permanent settlers came as a group of their countrymen 300 miles to the east penned their names to something called the Declaration of Independence. Native-born North Americans for the most part, the travelers carried their meager belongings on their backs and the backs of their mules and in the crude wagons they pulled. No artisans were they, but strong woodsmen. Brave men. Men who fought as they moved—fought the Indians, fought the howling wilderness. Kentucky, they learned from the red man, was the "Dark and Bloody Ground." They survived in it only because they were as savage and rugged as the land itself.

Their past was best forgotten. A race of blondes and redheads, they were once the commoners of Great Britain, descendants of the ancient Saxons, Celts, Angles and Norse invaders of Scotland and Ireland. Poverty and oppression forced them from eighteenth-century Europe to America. Some, the outcasts of debtors prisons, came as indentured servants and were set to work on coastal plantations until they could escape inland. When others of better means landed at Baltimore, Philadelphia, Savannah or Charleston, they found that earlier arrivals already possessed the land. So they moved westward, up river valleys like the Shenandoah, almost to the eastern slopes of the Appalachian Mountains. Here they gave birth to a new generation, which grew up knowing only the ways of the backwoods.

Boone was one of these men, and if one were to believe television, he conquered the frontier single-handedly. Actually, Boone, a persistent ne'er-do-well who deserted his family for months at a time, was a latecomer. Other "long hunters" had discovered Cumberland Gap 19 years before he first visited it in 1769, and if it hadn't been for the writings of his biographer John Filson, a schoolteacher turned land speculator, Ol' Dan'l would have passed into antiquity with nary a mention.

The long hunters and those who followed them into the mountains for the next half century were restless men. They hungered for open, virgin land and a life free from even the most rudimentary social controls. The lure of free land and plentiful game drew some of them to Appalachia. Others came to claim land tracts deeded to them for their Revolutionary War service. Still others simply stopped on their way westward and never bothered to move on.

Their settlement was haphazard, quite unlike that in the seaboard states, where whole towns and busy plantations sprang up soon after the first boats arrived. But the frontiersman wasn't interested in building cities; he wanted to get away from them. His family traveled the wilderness paths alone, or in small groups. When they became too tired to go any farther, or found an unoccupied piece of land that looked inviting, the leader of the group simply plopped down his musket. That was that. Here the family would build their log cabin or lean-to and raise their gigantic brood of children, living by scratch farming, hunting and making moonshine whiskey.

It was an uncomplicated life. But the land failed to live up to expectations. Except in the rich bottomlands of the region's rivers—the New River, the Big Sandy, the Cumberland and the Kentucky—the land yielded only the barest of crops, and it constantly suffered under extremes of heat and cold, flood and drought. Most fatally, it trapped the settlers in, isolated them from one another. It kept visitors and new ideas away for more than a century, leaving its settlers guileless children who even into the first decades of the twentieth-century lived under pioneer conditions, eating sowbelly and greens. A people easy to exploit, easy to promise to, easy to betray.

And there were many promises. Each one broken added anew to the plight of the Appalachian highlander.

There was the promise of education—but the under-financed schools, often staffed by teachers without even a high school diploma, have left the region with the nation's highest illiteracy rate and the average mountaineer with only a sixth-grade education.

There was the promise of politics—but the breast-beating politicians who doted on praising the fiercely independent virtues of "America's purest Anglo-Saxon stock" were too timid, or too corrupt, to help them by taxing the riches that flowed from their hills to corporate coffers in Pittsburgh, Cleveland and New York.

There was the promise of the richness of nature—but the great stands of virgin timber were bought and destroyed for scandalously few dollars by outside timber speculators, and the mineral rights were purchased from unsuspecting mountaineers for pennies (usually 50 cents an acre) by slick-talking land-company agents under broad-form deeds giving them for all time a claim to gouge at the vast underground stores of coal.

And there was the biggest promise of all, the promise of coal—but the black gold that brought the region its only brief periods of prosperity eventually left its people mangled and jobless.

By 1960 coal was on its hardest days. Scores of mines had shut down, thousands of miners were in unemployment lines. Hundreds more had fled to Detroit, Chicago and Dayton. Two promises were held out for those who remained. The first was the United Mine Workers union, the only mass-reform group the region had ever known, an organization that had given coal diggers dignity and decent wages in the past. The second was the response of an outraged nation—an untested oddity that came to be called "The War on Poverty." Both failed but for different reasons: the UMW because it became hopelessly enmeshed in corruption; the War on Poverty because it offered too little in too short a time without enough understanding of the unique forces that had shaped Appalachia into the nation's poorest region.

The chapters that follow are my search for why they failed. They are written as a notebook. Their viewpoint is one of a journalist—a voyeur, as Gay Talese has said, who can see the warts on the world. Their primary theme is the Appalachian coal miner, the tragedy of his life. Their biases are those of a student who lived in Washington during the days when the Great Society was born and came to believe in its promises, and those of a traveler worn weary by driving too many miles over narrow mountain roads—15,000 in the last year alone—and hearing one old man one day say, "muleshit."

3

The Union, a New Hope

It was a chilly, moonless night in the late winter of 1931 when Red Poore and 110 other coal miners took the United Mine Workers of America "obligation" in Pounding Mill Hollow, Harlan County, Kentucky. He arrived alone. First one set of guards checked to see that his name was on their list and that he could be trusted; farther up the hollow, another set rechecked. Finally, he was waved forward to a third guardpost by a circling pinpoint of light that, he recalls, looked like a firefly.

Alone and by twos and threes more miners gathered. The darkness hid their faces. Just when the cold had seeped through Poore's denim jacket, W. B. Jones, a union organizer from Tennessee, climbed atop a stump. Within minutes all 111 coal diggers had taken the UMW's oath of brotherhood and committed themselves to what would become one of the bloodiest decades in the American labor movement.

It took courage to join the UMW in places like Harlan County during the big union drives of the 1930's. The Black Mountain Coal Company, where Poore worked, and every other coal company in the county were dead set against the union and had hired scores of "gun thugs" to enforce their edicts. Miners found to have joined the union were fired. Sometimes they were beaten. Their families were thrown out of company houses. Their names were placed on blacklists circulated throughout the coalfield. Chances of finding another job were slim.

Yet hundreds did join the union at clandestine meetings out of the sight of company law during a succession of organizing drives. The miners had little choice. The coal companies held an almost feudal stranglehold on their lives. The union was their only hope.

"Mining just didn't pay nothing," Poore said as we drove up Pounding Mill Hollow. "I was getting right about $2.86 a day and working only three-four days a week. I jumped at the union right quick. I tell you though, it was a rough son of a bitch. The thugs were everywhere. If they found out you were organizing they'd come to your house and beat the hell out of you."

The thugs never found out about Poore, then a strapping 25, and when the union called a strike in April, 1931, he joined it. Like the rest of the miners he watched the company evict union members from their homes and replace them with strikebreakers. Tempers had reached an explosive pitch by May 5, when the company sent a truck to nearby Verda for the furniture of a strikebreaker named Roy Hughes. Miners gathered by the score in the streets of Evarts, a "free town" between Verda and Black Mountain. Some had guns. All were angry. Harlan County Sheriff John Henry Blair, an ardent foe of the union, heard that the idle miners intended to stop Hughes on his return trip. (This was true, but the miners later said they simply wanted to plead with the strikebreaker to join them.) Blair telephoned Jim Daniels, a company-paid deputy sheriff at Black Mountain, and told him to take a bunch of mine guards to Evarts. Daniels and nine armed men set out in three autos. They drove cautiously through Evarts. It appeared tense but peaceful. Then at the edge of town all hell broke loose.

When the smoke cleared, the bodies of three mine guards and one miner were scattered on the roadway. The bodies of an undetermined number of other men were dragged away up the mountainside. Some say as many as ten more men may have died in what became known as "The Battle of Evarts." Who shot first was never determined. And whether Daniels and his men were on a deliberate mission to clear out the miners or were ambushed is a question buried in weeks of conflicting court testimony.

What is clear is that 43 men, all connected with the union in some way, were indicted after the battle. Fifteen trials eventually came up in a court system controlled by coal interests. Three ended in acquittals. Five ended in hung juries. Seven ended in convictions and life sentences for "conspiracy to murder." Red Poore, who still maintains he was in a store more than half a mile away when the shooting occurred, was one of them. He spent ten years in prison before receiving a governor's pardon. Today, he calls himself the only survivor of The Battle of Evarts, an episode that set the tenor of labor relations in Harlan County for nearly a decade.

"Bloody Harlan"

By 1931, Harlan County had a well-established reputation as "the toughest spot to unionize" in the country. For years it had been known as "bloody Harlan." It was, and continued to be, feud country. In 1938, Harlan County with fewer than 65,000 inhabitants had 75 murders; New York City with more than 7 million had only 61.

Shaped like a narrow coal shovel, the county nestles shoulder to shoulder with the Virginia border in the far southeastern corner of Kentucky. It was the last of the great coalfields to open, and until 1910 was a quiet collection of small mountain farms without even a railroad. Its chief industries were logging and farming—along with more than a little moonshining.

Coal changed everything. Tucked in easy-to-mine seams, it was too tempting to ignore. Dozens of local businessmen got into the act. They dug corridors into the hillsides and set as many men as they could gather to pick at the rich seams. The first carloads of what they called "Black Gold" left the county on the new Louisville & Nashville Railroad division in 1911. Experts said it was some of the highest quality bituminous, or soft, coal in the nation. The outbreak of World War I increased the demand for coal. Soon some of the nation's largest corporations joined the local operators. Eventually, U. S. Steel, International Harvester, Ford Motor and Peabody Coal all found their way to Bloody Harlan. So did thousands of mountaineers, many of them descendants of the rugged pioneers who first crossed the Cumberland Gap in the 1700's.

There were no towns, no stores, no houses for the new miners and their families—except those the coal operators built. Rows of four- and five-room shacks soon appeared near the entrance of every mine. The company town, the company store and company law came into being. Production soared, and the population with it. By 1930, the number of inhabitants in Harlan County had jumped sixfold in less than two decades. One-third of the coal mined in Kentucky came from county mines.

Harry Wallace

"Reckon I was in 'bout every scrape the union ever had in this here county," Harry Wallace said. "The only time I ever got lawed [arrested] was for the union. Happened three times."

Wallace, a miner for 52 years, was in his flower garden across the street from Evarts High School. The memories of his union-organizing days were still painfully vivid, too vivid —so much so he hesitated to tell them to a stranger. I coaxed him to continue. He did so reluctantly, as if afraid a company guard was still peering over his shoulder ready to bust his head at any false move.

His words were slow at first:

"Was lawed for signing men up with the union. Thrown out of my company house. Blacklisted too. Couldn't find a job for weeks. Would have been in bad shape, 'cept I was a good ballplayer, a catcher. In those days, all the companies had ball teams. I caught. My brother pitched. Got two jobs that way. After I was lawed from my third house, vowed I'd never live in a company house again. Never could buy though. Still rent. Never knew whether you'd have a job one day to the next."

Wallace joined the union in 1917. Harlan County went solidly UMW that year. It had to. During the war years, operators were forced by the Federal Fuel Administration to sign wage agreements with the UMW. Most of them, however, did not formally recognize the union, and after the war the agreements were discontinued. The Black Mountain Coal Company (a subsidiary of Peabody Coal), where Wallace worked off and on, opened in 1919 and signed a union contract. It became the only company in the county that would hire men with records of union activity. In 1921, the union again attempted to organize the county. It failed. And in 1924, the local at Black Mountain struck for higher wages and a new contract. After six months, its men went back to work. The union died out. It was 1933 before Black Mountain or any other county coal company recognized the UMW.

In the meantime, the depression hit Harlan County harder than most coal counties. It was farther from the major markets than other fields, and its freight rates were higher. The price of coal fell and with it wages. Coal operators who had lived and worked with their miners in mutual respect for almost two decades found themselves increasingly at odds with their men. Working hours lengthened and conditions deteriorated. Some companies went out of business. Other operators, who had always maintained a paternalistic attitude toward their employees, became increasingly domineering and resentful as their profits slid. Visiting newsmen found miners working for $4 and $5 a week, children going to school without lunch, looting commonplace and begging widespread.

Miners able to find work lived in utter peonage. They boarded their families in company houses. They shopped in company stores, strolled company streets and were paid in company scrip (company money good for trade only in company towns). Their children went to company schools. Their wives delivered their offspring in company hospitals attended by company doctors. And when they died they were buried in a company cemetery by a company undertaker. The costs of all these services, of course, were deducted from the miners' pay. Seldom was anything left over to buy even basic necessities, and miners sank further and further into debt—to the company—with each "payday."

Then came The Battle of Evarts, the National Guard, more

company paid "lawmen" and the entry of the communist-backed National Miners Union (NMU). Harlan County was thrust into the national spotlight. Within a few weeks, one news service reported: "War is on between Harlan County's thousands of jobless miners and the mine operators. Real war with machine guns and tear gas on one side against squirrel rifles on the other."

The entry of the NMU and an *ad hoc* investigating team of writers led by novelist Theodore Dreiser further incensed coal operators. Miners grasped for anything that offered help. Scores in Bell and Harlan Counties joined the communist union and ate free meals in its tent kitchens. A few tipples were dynamited and shots were fired at some operators.

"A man gets pretty desperate when he doesn't have a bag of flour for bread," Henry Wallace said. His spade pummeled the sandy soil around his dahlias. He tossed a chunk of dirt two feet in the air. It came down hard against the shovel blade and the wind took a whiff of it away in a tiny cloud of dust. Wallace let the rest fall back into the garden bed. He continued working silently.

Mine operators fought back with a reign of terror. Their leaders, a *New York Times* reporter found, feared "a revolt of miners this winter, instigated and led by the Communists and the IWW [Industrial Workers of the World]. By revolt I mean just that—revolution and a seizure of the reins of government." Most of the operators were mountaineers themselves, rugged individualists, self-made men. "Lot of them were just 10 or 12 years away from the shovel themselves," said one current operator. "They embodied all the self-righteousness that characterizes all self-made men. They were convinced they had to act." In any event, the revolt never took place, although there was more than a little bloodletting. Union membership fell rapidly, and by late 1932 no dues-paying UMW members were employed in Harlan County. The IWW and the NMU were rendered equally inoperative.

The Reign of Terror

A special committee appointed by Kentucky Governor Ruby Lafoon to investigate Harlan County troubles offered more than a hint of how this was done. A 1935 report on its findings said:

> It is almost unbelievable that anywhere in a free and democratic Nation such as ours, conditions can be found as bad as they are in Harlan County. There exists a virtual reign of terror, financed in general by a group of coal mine operators in collusion with certain public officials; the victims of terror are the coal miners and their families.
>
> In Harlan County we found a monster-like reign of oppression, whose tentacles reached into the very foundation of the social structure and even into the church of God. . . . Free speech and the right of peaceable assemblage is scarcely tolerated. Those who attend meetings or voice any sentiment favorable to organized labor are promptly discharged and evicted from their homes. Many are beaten and mistreated in most unjust and un-American methods by some operators using certain so-called peace officers to carry out their desires.

Coal operators, the commission concluded, failed to recognize that their employees were "human beings, with equal rights under the law with themselves." It recommended that the present system of deputized mine guards and one-sided administration of the law be abolished.

The report was ignored. It was not until after the passage of the National Labor Relations Act of 1935 and a second in-

vestigation, this one by a U.S. Senate subcommittee led by
Wisconsin Senator Robert LaFollette, that the UMW again
gained a foothold. And even then union organizing remained
a dangerous business.

January and February of 1937 offer good cases in point.
The union, which had renewed its organizing efforts, had
sent a group of paid organizers into the county. On January
11, they registered at the New Harlan Hotel. Before they
even unpacked, a friendly deputy sheriff dropped by to warn
them: "These fellows up here will kill you, they will dyna-
mite, they will shoot, they will burn you." The organizers
soon found out what he meant. L. T. Arnett, the leader of the
drive, told how company-paid deputy sheriffs put on the
pressure:

> . . . there were more deputy sheriffs than miners in Harlan
> County. We saw more of them than we did the miners. They
> just got thick everywhere.
> . . . they would come up to our people and jump out of
> their cars and come around and pull their guns from their
> hips around to the front, and talk rough and mean to them,
> and tell them to get out, get going, get on the highway and
> keep moving.

Later the going got really rough. One night tear-gas
bombs crashed through the windows of the organizers'
rooms, driving them into the streets. Another night their cars
were dynamited. On still another occasion, Arnett and three
assistants came on a car parked beside the road between the
towns of Verda and Ages as they returned from a union
meeting. Frank White, a deputy sheriff hired for his prowess
with the machine gun, was behind the wheel. As the union
car drew even with him, White blasted the horn twice. A
rain of bullets flew at the union men. One hit the car's radia-
tor. Another knocked Arnett's hat off. Another struck an or-

ganizer in the shoulder. A bullet ripped through a second union car and hit the driver in the upper leg. The drivers stomped the accelerators to the floor and careened down the narrow highway, swerving to miss piles of brush, tree stumps and wagon wheels which had been scattered in their path. The organizers left the county that night. One of their number was seriously wounded.

Marshall A. Musick, a preacher, former coal miner and union organizer, was a special target. He lived just outside Evarts with his wife and children. When the union drive started, he was assigned organizing duties in the central part of the county.

On Sunday, January 31, Musick and his wife were walking toward the main highway to catch a bus home after spending the afternoon with friends when they heard an auto horn. They turned, thinking it was a bus. All they could see were two cars stopped on the road nearby. Suddenly they were caught in a crossfire of gunshots. One bullet grazed Musick's neck. Another splattered mud and gravel on his wife. Nine days later he left town. He boarded a train for Pineville, the county seat of nearby Bell County, early that evening, thinking his family would be safe if he weren't there. When he arrived in Pineville, he found out that a barrage of bullets fired from passing cars had ripped through his living room. One had killed his 19-year-old son, Bennett.

Union men had little hope of protection from county officials. The Harlan County Coal Operators Association kept them, along with the county's law-enforcement and court systems, in its back pocket. The association used much of its muscle to combat unionism. It collected $438,795 from its 38 members between 1927 and 1938 to do so. Its hold on the political system was unbreakable. Association secretary George Ward was chairman of the Republican county committee; president S. J. Dickerson was chairman of the Democratic county committee.

When political persuasion didn't work, cash did. Commonwealth Attorney Daniel Boone Smith, for example, had done little to prosecute miners' grievances; three association members placed him on a lucrative retainer. High Sheriff Theodore Middleton, a former poolhall operator elected on a reform platform, found friendly relations with the coal bosses even more profitable. Mysteriously his net worth rose from about $10,000 to upward of $200,000 in three years in office. Three lucrative business deals with coal operators provided much of the gravy. County Judge Morris Saylor, the county's chief executive and judicial officer, was tied into the same deal, an aspect of which involved part ownership in a company store at a nonunion mining site. Investments by the two officials in the store paid 170 percent dividends its first year of operation. In another deal, a coal-association member arranged the purchase of mining property that guaranteed a $5,000 royalty payment each year.

Few dared challenge coal interests. One who did was County Attorney Elmon Middletown, who hinted that he planned to press for a grand jury investigation of the intimidation of miners. Before the investigation materialized, a bomb went off in Middletown's car. He was killed instantly.

Deputy Sheriff Ben Unthank's brute force was immense. In 1937, he could call on 369 deputies, 181 of them directly on the payrolls of coal companies. The deputies were an unsavory bunch, and law and order meant terror in Harlan County. Sixty-four of these "law officers" had been indicted by grand juries for various crimes; more than a few of the indictments were for murder. Three had served time in federal prisons; 37 in state prisons. The high sheriff himself had once gone to prison for bootlegging.

Badges didn't change their ways. Slemp Middletown, the sheriff's brother, for instance, was indicted six times during his two years as a deputy. At one point a judge described him as "one of the most dangerous men in Harlan County."

No one explained the role of these "lawmen" more vividly than Bill C. "Thug" Johnson, a professional roughneck the Harlan Wallins Coal Company brought to the county from West Virginia. Officially, Johnson was a "cut boss" whose job was to fire all union men from the company's mines. But Johnson spent most of his time "thugging." Asked what this meant, he told the LaFollette investigating committee:

"Out hunting for union men, organizers, etc., in Harlan County."

You meant hunting for them, in what way? Not as you would hunt deer?

"Well, I never did kill nobody—in Harlan County," Johnson said.

Tell us some of your experience in that kind of work?

"What they said we would do, we would catch them and take them out and bump them off," he said.

The Soap Opera Rebels

Tales of the thugs, the nightriders and the union still linger in Harlan County. The miners who were so much a part of it are old now. They spend their days on the front porches and post-office steps that dot almost every mining camp, waiting to die. Their memories are bitter.

"A lot of men were killed in this county over the union," Jim Carpenter, 76, will tell you as he watches his favorite morning soap opera. "It was worth every bit. Companies just don't have any feelings for a man or his family. The union, it's the only thing a poor man's got."

The battles and the secret union meetings seem like yesterday. The names of Unthank, Jones, Middleton, and dozens of others roll off the tongues as if their voices were still in the neighborhood. At LeJunior, Ben Forester, 81, recalls how Bennett Musick was murdered just down the road and how the union organizer who signed him on the UMW rolls had to sneak around before daylight.

"Finally they killed him too, over at Martin Fork. 'Bout two years later," he says. "We had to be rough, too, sometimes. Them thugs were rough with us. When a man would step across a picket line we'd throw him in the river—baptize him, we called it."

The miners tell how some coal bosses were fairminded. Others "didn't put an ounce worth in a human life." "They had men over on that hill working for a dollar a day," one will say. "I saw them in 1930 picking grass and weeds cuzz they didn't have nothing to eat."

The UMW is always the good guy in these conversations, its organizers the prophets chosen to lead the miners to the promised land. John L. Lewis, the late UMW president, is the patron saint, "the greatest labor leader this country ever saw," "the best friend a coal miner ever had." The fixation is almost religious, in a sense even deeper because religion never really caught on in most of Appalachia.

Some of it is economic. The union brought Harlan County some of the highest industrial wages in the country, a new modern hospital, free medical care for miners, a pension that enables them to retire at 55 and some security.

But mostly it's a memory of what was.

"Before the union, you just got one day older and deeper in debt," said Jess Gilbert, a battleworn veteran of the organizing days. "If it wasn't for the union, it would still be like 1931 here. It would just be slave labor.

"Yessir, the union made this here country."

4

The Fall

In his 35th year as president of the United Mine Workers union, John L. Lewis stomped into a Senate subcommittee hearing one day to denounce the "human jackals" in other unions who were pilfering their member's funds.

Congress ought to expose "some of those crooks" to their union members, he thundered. "I'd like to have you show me one crook in the United Mine Workers—and see what I'd do about it."

The year was 1955. Lewis the man and Lewis the legend were at their pinnacle. For years, Lewis had been denounced by presidents and idolized by members of the nation's most militant labor union. Now, everything was falling into place for him. The union he had built—some said single-handedly—was the pride of the American labor movement. Mine wages stood at almost as much an *hour* as they had been a *day* 20 years before. The welfare and pension fund that Lewis pioneered guaranteed union members free medical care and old-age assistance. And just opening were a string of union-owned hospitals that would revolutionize the primitive medical standards of Appalachia.

The cantankerous Lewis hadn't called a strike in five years. He had made amends with some old adversaries, such as Harry Truman, whom he had once described as a "malignant, scheming sort of individual." Coal operators were calling him "the foremost labor statesman of the world." And now senators, with whom he had tangled so many times before, were seeking his advice on how to control corruption in the welfare funds of other unions.

Time and the union changed. Lewis himself lived 14 more years. But by his death in June, 1969, his biographer Saul Alinski wrote, "He survived his life and that of his enemies, and with a few exceptions, his friends, his allies and in a significant sense, his union and the world he had known."

Tragically, the year after his death found the UMW enmeshed in the same corruption that Lewis warned against so eloquently that November day in 1955. The brutal slaying of Joseph A. Yablonski, who had challenged Lewis' handpicked successor, tainted its very existence. The FBI, the Internal Revenue Service, the departments of Labor and Justice, and a Senate subcommittee all undertook separate probes. No union had come under such rigorous scrutiny since the days of teamster boss Jimmy Hoffa. And none deserved it more.

Institutions, unlike ladies, don't lose their honor in a night. They rust from within. The men who run them grow old. They lose their zeal and sense of purpose. Old battles are won, and ungrateful critics forget about them. Bureaucracies build up to perform the services the battles were all about. Often they perform well and become an end in themselves.

Circumstances dictate decisions. Promises of the past are found to be overstated or hard to deliver. New battles are avoided. Leaders pass. Direction is lost. A state of limbo develops. Self-interest becomes more important than group concern. The disease festers and sometimes the symptoms are noticed only from the outside. Such is the case of the UMW.

The pattern should easily have been discerned during the early 1960's, but, for the most part, it wasn't. For more than two decades, the union had reigned supreme in central Appalachia. Its strikes controlled production; its influence decided elections. Its candidates replaced those of the discredited coal operators in dozens of courthouses, ending the near-feudal state of coalcamp life.

But when Lewis, the master tactician and guru for thousands of miners, retired, he left in his place a bunch of unimaginative union stalwarts. The coal industry had just completed the most turbulent decade in its history and was locked in feverous competition with cheaper fuels. Mechanization, a product of the competition, had put miners out of work. Unemployment, sometimes exceeding 30 percent, was a brutal fact of life throughout the coalfields. Union membership waned as thousands of miners were left jobless. The UMW Health and Welfare Fund found itself overextended; four times in ten years its trustees rewrote eligibility requirements, cutting off tens of thousands of miners and their widows from its benefits.

The fall was underway, yet miners remained loyal. Hundreds who had lost their jobs continued paying membership dues. They were confident the union that had delivered on so many previous occasions would not fail them now.

The coal industry would recover, they said to themselves. The union would organize the scores of nonunion "doghole" mines that men had been forced to work in to support their families.

But it didn't. In the words of Appalachian author and social critic Harry Caudill, "The United Mine Workers of America abandoned the region." Miners found out about it during the summer and fall of 1962 in tersely worded letters from union headquarters. Their memberships and welfare cards had been canceled because their employers were not living up to the contracts they had signed with the union, the letters said. Specifically, most were behind in their payments to the welfare fund. A short time later the welfare-fund trustees unceremoniously announced they would close four of the ultramodern hospitals the union had built unless a nonprofit corporation could be found to buy them.

Miners were baffled. They had fought for the union; many had risked their lives. They felt closer to it than to any other institution. For many, it was their religion, their most prized asset. Now with hardly a forewarning it deserted them without even giving them a hearing. Few knew that their employers hadn't kept up—or in fact couldn't afford to keep up and stay in business—with their payments to the welfare fund. The union had never made a point of it before. Each miner suffered in his own way.

"It hurt me inwardly," Bryan Dixon, a 74-year-old former miner who lives on Elk Creek near Blackey, Kentucky, told me one day in late autumn. "I never did nothing wrong as as far as dishonesty, or taking something from someone, or bootlegging. I raised my family and always tried to do right by them. And then to think I was laid down like that. It really hurt. To think they laid down on a man who had put up dues and been loyal all that time."

Dixon grimly clutched the knee of his gray work pants as he spoke. His knuckles were white with emotion. His right thumb was missing, a casualty of a mine accident years before. Dixon mined for 42 years and was a charter member of his UMW local. In 1959, he retired, "thinking me and the old lady would be secure in our old age with our union pension." However, his request for the pension was denied for reasons he is still unsure of. Two years later the union took away the card that entitled him to free medical benefits, and a local union official told him it was fruitless to keep paying union dues.

"I spent my whole life between two rocks with bad water and bad air, then they come and throwed me out," Dixon said. "I didn't think I'd ever need anything more than the UMW. It damaged my whole life. Not only then, but now. I don't guess I'll ever get over it."

He paused. I started to leave, but Dixon stopped me. "I don't have any regrets standing up for the union, now understand," he said. "It's the only thing a working man's got. But I'd tell my story in Washington before Tony Boyle and John Owens if I had a chance. Millions of dollars been wasted that should have gone to miners like me, because we worked for it."

Tony Boyle

William Anthony "Tony" Boyle is president of the UMW. John Owens is secretary-treasurer. As far as Dixon remembers, neither has ever visited Blackey. Nor is it likely that they ever will. For one thing, only a handful of dues-paying members, most of them retired, remain in the community.

Once there were hundreds. For another, Blackey is a tiny backwater ghost town 723 miles from the plush former men's club that houses the UMW headquarters in downtown Washington, D.C. Finally, in recent years the pair has ventured into coalfields ever less frequently.

Their wants are well cared for in Washington. Boyle collects an annual salary of $50,000 (in 1968, he modestly refused an offer to double that); Owens gets $40,000—the same as Boyle's executive assistant Suzanne Richards, a bossy spinster who many say runs the union. Then there are the "fringe benefits": the chauffeured Cadillacs; the expense accounts (Boyle claimed $11,630 in 1967, Owens $4,945, but that didn't count an $11,500 hotel bill that the union paid from another account); and a very special retirement plan.

In the unlikely event that Boyle or Owens should ever decide to retire, they have thoughtfully provided for their own well-being by diverting $1.5 million in union money to a retirement fund without telling the membership about it. While miners collect $150-a-month pensions when they retire, the special fund will enable the pair to retire at full pay.

Nor do Boyle and Owens need worry about their kinfolk catching a bus for Detroit or Chicago to look for work as do the former union members in Blackey. Boyle's only daughter, Antoinette, a divorcee with one child, receives $40,000 a year as a UMW attorney in Billings, Montana, an area with few miners and little union legal work. His brother, R. J. Boyle, serves as an appointed district union official in the same area. His salary and expenses totaled $36,174 in 1968. Secretary-treasurer Owens has two sons on the union payroll: one at $40,000, the other at $25,000. But he and Boyle are pikers compared to another high union official, Harrison Combs, Sr. He has had three sons, one son-in-law and one daughter-in-law on union dole. Combs' family cost the union $132,000 in 1967.

Millions (one federal court decision estimated $9 million) have been squandered on questionable grants and loans, bad investments and foolhardy self-aggrandizement. Staggering amounts that should have been used for the benefit of miners and their widows have been lost through misuse and ineptitude. A 1969 Department of Labor audit, for example, found the union hadn't required documentation for more than $1 million dispersed in expense accounts to union officials, a violation of federal labor law. So loose were accounting procedures that one official regularly collected $20 a day while on vacation, and countless others claimed travel expenses without ever leaving home. "Some officials have claimed expenses for hotel and travel for practically every day of the year," the report commented.

Nor did UMW officials show much more diligence in handling union reserves. Until early 1970, the union Health and Welfare Fund kept from $20 million to $100 million in a non-interest-drawing checking account at the union-owned bank "for reasons of nervousness." At even a modest 5 percent return, the money would have earned up to $5 million in interest annually. Union financiers have done worse. During the stock market boom years of the 1960's, the union's $30.7-million stock portfolio showed an astonishing loss of $7 million.

It probably is just as well. If the money hadn't been lost, it might have been used for the self-glorification of Tony Boyle, who encourages the most embarrassing displays of hero worship from underlings. (One 24-page issue of the UMW *Journal*, the official union newspaper, carried 28 Boyle photos). In the five-year period beginning in 1963, for instance, the union bought $93,375 worth of photos of the union president and his cronies. In 1968, more than $100,000 was spent on "Boyle" cigarette lighters, clocks, gavels and pens distributed at the union's convention. The union hired two little-known bands for $200,000 (it had paid five bands $390,000 in 1964) for the same meeting. One of their jobs was to play a new composition—"The Ballad of Tony Boyle." One delegate recalls that after "they had played it a couple of hundred times," the membership generously offered to double Boyle's salary and give him a lifetime appointment. He refused, saying he wanted to preserve the union's democratic processes.

Miners have little to say about how their union is run, their money spent.

Technically, their best chance should be at the union's conventions, held once every four years. Boyle has called the conventions "more democratic than the United States Congress." Hardly. For one thing, the two since he took office have been held far from the coalfields (in Denver and Miami), making it difficult for working miners to attend. For another, they have been stacked with his supporters, many holding one or more of the 500-odd $60-a-day convention jobs. Many of these jobs are political plums with few, if any, real responsibilities. In 1968, for instance, the 39 members of the Appeals and Grievance Committee were paid $40,800. Yet there were no grievances or appeals.

Meaningful discussion is squelched in the most brutal manner. Controversial resolutions are mysteriously lost. Delegates who question policy and procedures are intimidated. At the 1964 convention, Louis Antal, a miner from Arnold, Pennsylvania, watched as another delegate tried to object to the seating of a coal-company official on the convention floor. "White helmets came from all over the floor of the convention," he recalled. "One gentleman had about 15 men on him, pounding him. They eventually took him out. He was bleeding like a stuck hog." The assailants were part of a well-known "goon squad" from eastern Kentucky and northern Tennessee. They wore miners' hardhats with the inscription "District 19—Boyle."

Miners fare little better at home. Their union is made up of 193,000 active and retired miners in 27 states and 4 Canadian provinces. Under the Landrum-Griffin Act of 1959, all union members must be given the right to elect their own representatives. But not so in the UMW. Boyle appoints the officers in 20 of the 25 geographical districts. Not a single miner in West Virginia, the nation's largest coal-producing state, for instance, has a voice in electing his district officials. The appointees, almost to a man, are extreme Boyle loyalists, old union stalwarts who have proven they can be trusted to carry out dictates from Washington. Many are over 65 and have little contact with working miners. As a result, such bitterness has arisen that rank-and-file members in some parts of West Virginia have warned the appointed district officers to stay out or face prospects of violence.

Another sore spot is the proliferation of illegal "bogus" unions. The union's constitution specifically provides that each local union must contain ten or more working miners. Yet the UMW leadership has blinked at this rule as coal companies have abandoned scores of mines, leaving many areas without any working miners. Today as many as 600 locals are bogus. The reasons are twofold, according to Karl Kafton, an outspoken Moundsville, West Virginia, miner: "One, to control the convention, and another, to control the elections and keep the incumbents entrenched. The bogus locals are easy votes to control. They don't want to lose them. I tell you the Czars of Russia could have learned something about tyranny from the leadership of the United Mine Workers union." There is little hope that this will change.

Lewis' Legacy

This is not to say that all that ails the UMW is the fault of President Boyle. He's simply the most visible symbol of a decadent system that has lost sight of its goals. Many of the men in the system aren't necessarily evil—just antiquated. They are men who have spent their lives with the union, nurtured and fought for it, men who learned to think of it as their personal property and, when it had grown fat, felt the dividends were rightfully theirs. So they took them, spread them to their families and sincerely felt hurt when someone had the audacity to question their motives. And when someone did, they reacted in the same way that they had in the Lewis heydays, not realizing that they were now the oppressors, the new coal barons, and not the fiery radicals of old.

It was Lewis who first brought William Anthony Boyle to Washington in 1948 as his administrative assistant and protégé. The dapper five-foot-six Irishman had been a coal miner in his native Montana until eight years before, when he was elected president of the union district. Adept at office politics, he proved a loyal servant to Lewis, doing what was asked of him and more, gradually rising in esteem among old union stalwarts. When Lewis retired, Boyle became vice-president. Three years later he was named president, succeeding Thomas Kennedy, who had died.

The organization Boyle inherited was geared to another generation and saddled with Lewis' aging cronies. Lewis had been a nineteenth-century man, a rare, self-educated creature who recited scripture and Shakespeare with ease. He built the union around himself and held complete dictatorial control over it. He kept its records in his head. He moved with events, sometimes changing allegiances and positions in midstream without telling his closest associates. And always there was a continuing passion for power. Those who helped him get it were rewarded; those who didn't were chastised. Dissent seldom went long unchecked. Nepotism and hidden financial deals flourished. "If you can't trust your relatives, who can you trust," he once told a UMW official, acknowledging that he had 17 relatives on the union payroll. Decision-making was his, and his alone. Eventually bright young leaders saw they had no future in the organization and drifted away. Those who remained grew old and retained the ideas of another era.

In 1963, the UMW needed dynamic leadership. Boyle offered little as its new president. When he moved, he moved slowly. He dared not offend the retired chieftain or his supporters. Lewis had retained two key posts—he was union trustee on the Health and Welfare Fund and president emeritus—and still kept a close eye on affairs from his mansion in nearby Virginia. The coal industry was on the verge of recovery. Soon it would be in the midst of a new boom. Coal companies would be rich but would employ thousands fewer miners. It was time for creative new programs to aid displaced union members and for a realignment of the Welfare Fund. Boyle, however, clung to old Lewis policies formulated while the industry was on its deathbed.

Most of the rank and file accepted Boyle because he was Lewis's man, and Lewis could do no wrong. Although union membership had dropped by more than half in the decade, wages for those miners with jobs continued to be high. Few thought to question the new regime. "We were too busy making car payments and feeding our kids to think about whether the union was stealing us blind or not," one miner told me.

Among dissidents, it was quite a different story. There Boyle had a well-established reputation for doing Lewis's dirty work. They feared his ruthlessness. The roots of their suspicions are best found in a bizarre 1951 court case. Charles Minton, a former UMW field worker, sued the union, for $350,000, alleging that he had been fired for refusing a Boyle order to murder two nonunion coal operators. Free legal help and a hefty payoff were supposedly part of the deal. The union didn't contest the charges, and their validity may never be known. A judge dismissed the case after Minton received an out-of-court settlement from the union. (In 1970, Boyle denied any involvement in the case. "That was before my time," he said at a rare press conference.)

Even among his supporters, however, there was no question that Boyle lacked the charisma, intellect and ties to the rank and file that had served Lewis so well. Anyone would suffer by comparison. But Boyle, short-tempered (he once threatened to stuff a bologna down the throat of West Virginia Congressman Ken Hechler) and plagued by what one UMW official called "a habit of sticking his foot in his mouth," magnified his own inadequacies. No matter how much he tried to sound like Lewis or evoke his memory, he always came out sounding like a bumbling small-town used-car salesman.

At no time did Boyle look worse than after a 1968 mine explosion killed 78 miners at Consolidation Coal Company's Mountaineer No. 9 mine near Farmington, West Virginia. While mourners still clung together outside the mine, Boyle praised Consol as a "cooperative" and safety-minded firm. "There is always this inherent danger in coal mining," he said, emphasizing that Consol is "one of the better companies to work with."

Boyle neglected to mention that this same mine had been found in violation of federal regulations in all two dozen inspections that the U.S. Bureau of Mines had made since

1963 and had been cited with 25 other safety violations in the preceeding two years.

Mrs. Judy Henderson was one of the widows who witnessed Boyle on the evening news. Then only 21, she had grown up in coal country and she knew of mine dangers. As children she and her future husband, Paul, had played on the grounds leading to the mine and had watched when an earlier explosion took 16 lives in 1954. Now Paul was dead and Boyle's statements were more than she could stomach.

"I hated him right then," she recalls. "I couldn't believe someone could say that right there in front of the mine where all our husbands were buried alive."

Paul Henderson, who was just 24, had frequently complained "how the union hadn't done anything for miners in 20 years," she said. "He was mad at the union, even his father and the local union members, for not speaking up about safety. Now I know what he was talking about."

So did a lot of other people, particularly critics like Congressman Ken Hechler and consumer crusader Ralph Nadar. For months they had maintained that the union hierarchy was more interested in coal production than in the safety of union members. Boyle's statements illustrated that more than anything else could. Actually, the union had worked closely with coal companies since 1950, when John L. Lewis committed his membership to encouraging the mechanization of mines. Indeed, its Health and Welfare Fund, which is financed by a levy on every ton of coal mined, gave the union a vested interest in production. The question thus became, had the union's cooperation with coal companies worked against the health and safety of miners? Critics said it had. Union leaders, of course, denied it.

The union's actual record on mine safety is less than spectacular. Only three times (1940, 1952 and 1969) during the last three decades has it persuaded Congress to adopt major mine-safety legislation, and it succeeded each time only after a disaster had killed dozens of miners. Some have wondered how serious the union has been about the subject. In 1968, at the time of the Farmington disaster, for example, the UMW employed only one safety expert in its Washington headquarters, and its district offices reported spending only $14 on safety education during the year in all West Virginia. The same year the union paid $75,000 to the National Coal Policy Conference, an industry-union lobbying group, to help promote the glories of coal production.

The toll of dead and maimed men has continued unabated. Coal mining remains the nation's most dangerous industrial occupation, an occupation four times as dangerous as trucking, two-and-a-half times as perilous as lumbering. In fact, some evidence suggests that it is getting more, rather than less, dangerous, despite the tough 1969 federal mine-safety law. In 1970, for instance, 234 men died in mine accidents, compared with 203 in 1969. Mine accidents have injured a total of 1.5 million men since 1930, and even today a young man going to work in the mines can expect to be put out of work as a result of accidents four or five times before he retires. Equally frightening is the fact that 1 miner in 12 who enters a mine in his early years can expect to be killed in an underground accident before he reaches retirement.

Still another grisly statistic is contained in a 1967 U.S. Surgeon General's report. It estimated that more than 100,000 current and former miners suffer from coal miners' pneumoconiosis, more commonly called "black lung." A painful, often fatal disease, black lung is caused by breathing the coal and rock dust found in mines. It coats the miner's lungs, cuts his breath short and causes him to cough up lumps of black sputum. Such routine tasks as climbing a few steps or walking up a hill become nearly impossible.

Although Great Britain had recognized black lung as an occupational disease for 26 years, and one of the UMW's own doctors had published articles about it as early as 1956, union policy makers did nothing about it until three West Virginia doctors started barnstorming the coalfields in 1968, awakening miners to its dangers. Even then, rather than joining the doctors—Donald Rasmussen, I. E. Buff and Hawley Wells—Boyle condemned them and threatened miners who joined them with expulsion from the union. "We're not going to destroy the coal industry to satisfy the frantic rantings of self-appointed and ill-informed saviors of coal miners," he said.

Nonetheless, 40,000 West Virginia miners walked off their jobs in a wildcat strike to support legislation drafted by the newly formed Black Lung Association. Boyle ordered them back to work. They refused, and when hundreds of them marched by union headquarters in Charlestown, they booed and raised their clenched fists in anger. Boyle pouted. Finally, after the strike had continued three weeks, legislators, with belated union support, passed a bill that made it possible for black-lung victims to receive assistance under the state's workmen's-compensation laws. Said Dr. Buff: "I think there is going to be an entire change in the state. For the first time the ordinary coal miner is free. Now he knows what he can do when he joins with other miners."

5

The Arrangement

Two days before Christmas 1950, beetlebrowed John Llewellyn Lewis strolled out of the Carleton Hotel in Washington, across 16th Street NW and into the new offices of one Harry Moses.

He wanted to see Moses, he announced to the secretary.

"Mr. Moses isn't in," she said. "Gone to Pittsburgh for the holidays. Any message?"

"Have him call me when he gets back," Lewis said. "But tell him there is no hurry."

With that, the 71-year-old Lewis strode out. He seldom made idle visits. In fact, he seldom made visits of any kind to old coal barons like Harry Moses. When he did, it was all business. Invariably that meant higher wages for his union members, and he preferred the coal barons to come to him in his office as he sat securely atop the nation's coal pile, or at least to meet him on neutral ground with newsreel cameras looking on, sometimes for weeks on end.

This year it was different. Six months earlier a group of powerful Northern and Western coal companies had banded together to form the Bituminous Coal Operators Association (BCOA). They hired Harry Moses to head the new BCOA for $65,000 a year with instructions to "stabilize our relationship" with the mine union. The coal companies, representing the giants of the industry, were particularly interested in getting wage negotiations "out of the klieg lights" and into the conference room, away from the annoying public and the federal government.

Moses, formerly president of H. C. Frick Coke Company, a subsidiary of U.S. Steel, worked rapidly. He found his old friend John L. Lewis, who only months before described all coal operators as "cruel, conscienceless men," surprisingly cooperative. The operators and the union gradually moved closer together. On December 27, Moses stopped the union president while he lunched at the Carleton. They chatted briefly. Ten days later the two men reached an informal wage agreement, which their respective groups rubber-stamped within the week. To practically everyone's surprise—everyone, that is, except Lewis and a tight inner circle of some of the nation's wealthiest coal executives—they had negotiated a nationwide agreement in complete secrecy, without a damaging strike, without messy headlines.

What Lewis and these men knew that the public and the nation's miners did not know was that secretly and somewhat mysteriously the union and the giants of the coal industry had arrived at an "arrangement" nine months earlier in signing the National Bituminous Coal Wage Agreement of 1950. Lewis only hinted that something out of the ordinary had occurred at the time. "The country is now freed from any thought of a so-called crisis for an indefinite period of time," he said without explanation.

The arrangement, however, abruptly changed the coal industry. In one swoop, gone were the costly nationwide strikes that had plagued the industry almost yearly. Gone were the angry bargaining sessions. In their place, a permanent peace settled over the industry, one that made it possible for Lewis and Moses to settle their differences quietly in 1951, one that reigned until the fall of 1971, more than 20 years later.

The 1950 agreement, union and industry spokesmen would later claim, was designed to stabilize the troubled coal industry, then in the throes of a life-and-death struggle for survival in the energy market with oil and natural-gas products. John L. Lewis, they said, had saved the industry from certain ruin by performing the statesmanlike action of tacitly giving his blessing to massive mechanization of the nation's mines.

What had actually happened, however, is that big labor and big management had joined in one of the most unusual and sinister alliances in the history of the American free-enterprise system. The alliance, two federal court juries have found, was a "continuing conspiracy" to drive hundreds of small mining concerns out of business—and thus throw thousands of miners out of their jobs.

Evidence of the conspiracy isn't found in any union documents or in the account books of any large corporation. After all, one hardly calls a press conference to announce that "we hereby agree to conspire" to do this or that. John Rowntree, the Knoxville lawyer who has made the conspiracy cases a personal crusade for a decade, says the real evidence of its existence is in "the effects of the course of conduct" after the 1950 National Bituminous Coal Agreement.

The effects are easy to see in places like the Kentucky coalfields: the coalcamps with the forlorn look of shelled cities; the mine offices with the boarded-up windows; the abandoned mines; the half-deserted rows of houses; the widows; and the men who haven't worked for 20 years.

The Matchmakers

As pieced together from three lawsuits, the arrangement that caused this decline has two central characters. One is Lewis, president of the UMW from 1920 to 1960 and perhaps the greatest labor leader of his age. The other is a lesser-known but equally powerful figure, George Love, former president of Consolidation Coal Company and in 1950 the chief labor negotiator for the large Northern coal interests.

Theirs was an unlikely match. Love, bald and debonair, was a graduate of Phillips Exeter Academy, Princeton and Harvard Business School. Lewis, the son of a Welch immigrant miner, went to work in a coal mine when he was only 15 and never bothered to finish eighth grade. In 1950, Love was 50 and unknown outside business circles. Lewis was 70, and for 30 years his stinging oratory and bushy locks had been synonomous with labor trouble. He had built the UMW, from near extinction in 1920, into the nation's most formidable labor organization. In the process, he founded and then abandoned the CIO (Congress of Industrial Organizations), openly defied two Democratic presidents friendly to labor, and made his miners the nation's highest-paid industrial workers.

In those days, coal was king. It heated more than half of all American homes and drove more than 95 percent of its railroad locomotives. It was, and is, essential for the production of steel and a host of chemical products, ranging from saccharin to plastic, from aspirin to perfume. Its energy powered most of the nation's industries and produced much of its electrical power.

A nationwide coal-diggers' strike could paralyze all this and send tremors through the entire economy for months, much as an industry-wide autoworkers' strike would do today. Thus, contract negotiations between the union and the coal operators were awaited with all the anticipation of a fight with a fickle mother-in-law. Lewis, once the manager of an opera house, never failed to dish up a good show.

Until 1950, the UMW negotiated separate contracts with three major groups, each representing a large segment of the coal industry. The contracts could take into account regional differences in wages, distance from markets, transportation costs and the types of coal seams worked. And each group could vie for a separate settlement. Lewis handled bargaining with the Northern Coal Operators Association, the largest single group, representing coal interests in Pennsylvania, northern West Virginia, Ohio, Illinois and western Kentucky. UMW vice-president Tom Kennedy, a former lieutenant-governor of Pennsylvania, negotiated with the captive mines, those directly owned by steel companies. Secretary-treasurer John Owens, who first went to work in the mines when he was ten years old, dealt with the Southern Coal Producers Association, traditionally the least cohesive group, representing coal companies in eastern Kentucky, Tennessee, Alabama, Virginia and southern West Virginia.

Negotiations with the Northern operators were invariably the loudest and longest because their settlements set the pace for the industry. For almost 20 years, Lewis' chief adversary in these sessions was Charles O'Neil, the cantankerous president of the Pennsylvania Coal Operators Association. Like Lewis, O'Neil was heavy-set and bushy-haired.

And like Lewis, he had a flair for the dramatic. While Lewis would bemoan the plight of his hapless coal diggers if union demands were not met, O'Neil would forecast doom for the coal industry and cold winter nights for old ladies if union demands were met. Newspapers of the day relished the encounters and tended to picture the bargaining sessions as gigantic alley fights between two powerful tomcats, with the national economy at stake. These accounts generally cast the union president as the bully in the match, but for years the UMW enjoyed the notoriety, for it gave Lewis a bigger-than-life image and built an unusual solidarity in the union.

The Change

By 1950, Lewis was on the verge of an abrupt about-face. The years of constant combat had obviously begun to wear on him. His old rival, Charlie O'Neil, was dead, and signs that bad days were coming for the coal industry were everywhere. In his public statements, Lewis maintained his old hard-nosed posture. "When evil days come upon this industry you will find the UMW moving in, and if there are only three work days in this industry, we will have three days work," he warned early that year. "If we are going to starve, we will just starve together."

George Love replaced O'Neil at the bargaining sessions. Love was cast from a different mold. He disliked publicity. While Love claimed to be no match for Lewis, behind the scenes he, suave and self-confident, was the industry's shrewdest arm-twister. Just two decades earlier Love had taken over his family's faltering coal company and converted it into a moneymaker almost overnight. By 1943, he moved to Consolidation Coal Company, then still recovering from a Depression bankruptcy. Consol, as the company is known in coal circles, had lost $100 million in the previous 15 years.

Under Love's leadership, it showed a $6-million profit in the first 12 months. Within two more years, Love—with the help of his close friend George Humphrey, later Eisenhower's Secretary of the Treasury—gained control of Consol and built it into the nation's largest coal combine through a series of mergers.

As it emerges from his actions and public statements, Love's overriding philosophy was that the only way coal could compete with other fuels was through revolution in its production methods. "We need to get away from the old type mine, to put in more and better machines, to get more talented men, and put mining on an assembly line basis," he told *Life* magazine in January, 1950. "It is a question of revitalizing an industry that hasn't been able to plan."

In an industry where labor often accounted for as much as 75 percent of total production costs, Love's statements made good business sense. But they ran directly counter to what John L. Lewis had preached for 30 years. His goal during those years had been the employment of the maximum number of miners at the highest wage levels possible. As late as 1949, he showed no affection for Love, calling him "a liar by the clock." That same year Lewis declared a series of three-day work weeks to insure that as many miners as possible found work. The work stoppages, the UMW *Journal* reported, were stabilization actions designed to keep the "big companies from hogging the market."

What, then, made Lewis abruptly change this policy in favor of one that clearly helped big companies "hog" the market and put thousands of his own miners out of work the next year, and signify this change by signing the National Bituminous Wage Agreement of 1950, is unclear.

Lewis' personal integrity is unquestionable. Perhaps he had grown battle weary. Perhaps he genuinely believed that massive mechanization was the only way to save the industry and his union. There is strong evidence to suggest he did. But, if so, it is hard to understand why no effort was made to retrain and relocate union members thrown out of work. Perhaps the increased contributions coal operators offered the Health and Welfare Fund, long Lewis' pet project, and the continual wage hikes were too tempting to resist. Or perhaps Lewis simply went along with George Love, not realizing the consequences.

In any event, by 1952 the arrangement was complete and Lewis was agreeing with Love that small coal operators were "just a drag on the industry" and should be phased out of business. In fact, as Lewis well knew, the process was well underway. In Kentucky alone the number of working mines decreased by one-half between 1950 and 1952. The number of employed miners dropped by 22,214, or almost one-third.

The Contract

What few realized is that the UMW contract, by approving repeated flat increases in wages and in contributions to the UMW Health and Welfare fund, was directly *responsible* for much of this cutback. The increases, in effect, made massive mechanization, which Lewis had once vigorously opposed, imperative.

In 1951 and each year thereafter, only two men negotiated the contracts: Lewis and a representative of the BCOA. They met secretly and drew up terms for the entire industry. After their respective groups rubber-stamped the agreement, the pair would announce it to the public and the nation's coal operators. The individual coal operator had little to say in the matter. There was only one contract for the industry; this was it. The operator could either accept it or reject it. If he rejected it, his workers would strike with UMW support and he would face the twin threat of union violence and a boycott by larger companies that had ratified the agreement. If he accepted it, at least he could stay in business, even if it meant eventual ruin.

For many smaller coal companies in eastern Kentucky, southern West Virginia and Tennessee, the contract did spell ruin. It increased wages $1.60 a day in 1951 and $1.90 a day in 1952. At the same time the levy for the union Health and Welfare Fund on every ton of coal produced increased from 20 cents in 1948 to 40 cents in 1952. Consumer coal prices remained stable in the meantime. Thus mines had to mechanize to stay in business. Large corporations, like Consolidated Coal, could afford to do this. Most smaller mines could not. Many of them dropped out of business.

If the arrangement wasn't good for them, it was very convenient for Consolidation Coal and George Love, who later testified he didn't like his competitors to pay wages lower than his if he "could do anything about it." Love designed the BCOA as an alliance between the big Northern coal operators and the captive mines owned by steel companies. Together the two groups mined about half the nation's coal, almost twice as much as the smaller mines in the South and clearly enough to dominate the traditionally fragmented coal industry.

As BCOA's architects, Love and Consol had a very special relationship with the bargaining group. Love modestly denies this, saying "we were one member of many." But actually Love controlled 52 of the 110 votes that could be cast on policy questions. If this wasn't enough to ramrod his wishes through every meeting, Love could turn to BCOA's president Harry Moses, whose election he engineered. Moses controlled U.S. Steel's 19 votes, giving the pair nearly a two-thirds majority. Given this situation, it is not hard to see how what was good for Consol and U.S. Steel became synonomous with what was good for the coal industry in the eyes of the BCOA.

Lewis the Coal Boss

While Love flexed his corporate muscle with the BCOA, his newfound ally Lewis was behaving rather strangely for a union leader. In the coalfields, UMW members had taken to the picket lines as part of a campaign to "organize every mine in this country." But in Washington, Lewis, the old management-baiter, was crossing the wide river that separates labor from management hand in hand with one of the nation's wealthiest industrialists. John L. Lewis was becoming a coal *operator.*

The UMW membership wasn't told that their union had gone into the coal business, or that their dues subsidized at least one large nonunion mine. When the details began to drift out later, the union hierarchy limply explained they had some "idle money" around. By their account the union invested in coal companies—along with two banks, a railroad and several utility firms—with the idea that it would increase job opportunities for union members.

However, an examination of the companies invested in raises serious doubt whether they actually produced any new jobs for miners or even enhanced jobs already in existence. The examination also fails to explain why the union loaned $1.5 million to North Fork Coal Company so it could purchase mineral leases in the Hazard, Kentucky, area. North Fork in turn leased the mining rights to the land to the Kentucky Oaks Mining Company, the largest nonunion strip-mining company in eastern Kentucky. Subsequently Kentucky Oaks, which the UMW had in effect subsidized, beat out several unionized firms in bidding for lucrative long-term contracts to provide coal to Tennessee Valley Authority (TVA) generating plants.

This leads to another, more cynical, explanation of why John L. Lewis became a coal operator, one advanced by small- and medium-sized coal companies in antitrust suits against the union and the giants of the coal industry: that the investments were part of a campaign to divide the rich TVA market among a handful of big companies.

The stakes in this campaign—waged with the UMW's blessing and treasury—were survival. In the depressed coal market of the early 1950's, the TVA offered one of the few stable markets in an otherwise shaky industry. A few years earlier the TVA had begun construction of a series of huge coal-burning generating plants. Originally the plants were designed to supply electricity to the Atomic Energy Commission projects at Oak Ridge, Tennessee. However, they soon expanded to other markets, constantly increasing their demands for coal. The TVA, like its counterparts in private industry, found it cheaper to buy this coal under long-term contracts. Soon these contracts became the most sought-after pieces of business in the nearby Southern coalfields.

None of this escaped John L. Lewis, coal operator. He saw the long-term importance of the TVA to both the industry and his union. Although the exact details are hazy, sometime in 1951 he summoned Cyrus Eaton, a wealthy Cleveland industrialist, to a meeting. Together they plotted how the UMW could gain a foothold in the TVA market. The vehicle they decided upon was the West Kentucky Coal Company, a nonunion firm with mines in three states. Without consulting the UMW membership, Lewis began funneling union funds to Eaton, then board chairman of the Chesapeake and Ohio Railway, so he could buy stock in West Kentucky Coal.

Within a year, UMW funds had purchased enough stock to earn Eaton a seat on the company's board of directors. Within two years, he became chairman of the board. His first act was to sign a UMW wage contract.

The takeover's immediate impact was to eliminate an embarrassing nonunion operation. But it was far more than an unorthodox organizing device, for it gave the union an entree into the TVA market, an entree that would prove invaluable in future years as it sought to set minimum-wage standards on all coal the agency purchased. Nor did the union's interest in West Kentucky Coal cease with the signing of the union contract in 1953. Lewis and Eaton continued their careers as coal operators for ten more years until the union canceled the loans and sold its West Kentucky stock to Island Creek Coal Company, another industrial giant, at a loss of $8 million in union funds. In the intervening years, the union had pumped a total of $25 million into the company, enabling it to capture 16 percent of the TVA market by operating at a loss.

The Squeeze Play

While this was going on, the BCOA had become worried about two developments George Love hadn't foreseen. One was the tendency of miners forced out of their jobs by mechanization to go to work in marginal "dog hole" mines at wages as low as $3 and $4 a day, thus flooding the market with cheap coal. Another was a series of "sweetheart" agreements the UMW had made with some unionized mines allowing them to pay less then their share into the UMW Health and Welfare Fund.

The BCOA moved to eliminate both problems in its 1958 bargaining session, held in even more than the usual secrecy. Their answer was a "protective wage clause," which pro-

hibited sweetheart deals and required all signatory companies to boycott coal mined by anyone not living up to the
union contract.

The protective wage clause was a crucial blow to scores
of self-made coal operators, among them Harry LaViers.
LaViers had been fighting the take-it-or-leave-it nationwide
contracts since 1951, instead favoring regional arrangements
that would take into consideration special regional problems.
Nevertheless, LaViers' South East Coal Company faithfully
paid union wages and kept up its 40-cents-a-ton contributions to the UMW Health and Welfare Fund, weathering
contract increases by investing in the most modern mining
machinery available.

By 1958, however, a recession had brought eastern Kentucky's economy to a near halt. Coal production fell to one-
third of what it had been eight years before; employment
dropped by two-thirds; and dozens of coal mines went out of
business. Those able to survive saw profits diminish as union
contracts increased manpower costs. Some dropped their
union affiliation, often despite threats of violence. Others,
like South East, stayed with the union but found competition
increasingly fierce.

South East had problems of its own. Two years earlier it
had embarked on an ambitious expansion program after it
found the coal reserves of its two Letcher County, Kentucky,
mines dangerously low. LaViers and his son, Harry, Jr., who
had become South East's general manager, had almost $2.5
million in cash at the time. They borrowed another $2
million and started work on a new mine and a coal-prepara-
tion plant. The mine was operating by August, 1958, but the
preparation plant proved much more costly than anticipated
and its opening was delayed.

In the meantime, Consolidation Coal and the UMW began
to put the squeeze on South East Coal, slowly at first, but

gradually tightening to a near stranglehold. It started when South East lost its sales agent and hired Consol to sell its coal at an 8-percent commission, 2 percent more than they had paid the old agent. Sales improved with Consol, but by 1961 South East was still operating in the red. The only way it could borrow more money to finish the preparation plant was to persuade Consol and the Louisville & Nashville Railroad to kick in $250,000 apiece. As a condition of the loan, George Love asked that Consol be given "a piece of the action." It was. Consol quickly brought 16 percent of South East's outstanding stock.

With a financial interest in South East, Consol could be expected to want to do anything it could to better South East's fortunes, if for no other reason than to insure its investment. Harry LaViers didn't think this unreasonable. In December, 1961, he went to Consol and told it that South East's UMW affiliation was slowly driving it broke. He wasn't idly poormouthing. In 1961, South East lost $250,000. At the same time it paid $215,000, or almost $1,000 per employee, to the union's Health and Welfare Fund. Only one of South East's 17 largest competitors paid that levy as well as the union wage scale, roughly 25 cents an hour higher than the going nonunion rate. LaViers told Consol that South East simply couldn't compete under these circumstances. Its union ties had to be severed.

No dice, said Consol. The "protective wage clause" would force Consol to discontinue selling South East's coal if South East canceled its union contract.

LaViers next journeyed to Washington to see Thomas Kennedy, who had succeeded John L. Lewis as UMW president. In a last effort to avoid a messy confrontation with the union and Consol, he hoped to convince Kennedy to modify South East's contract.

Kennedy would hear nothing of it. "You know we have a

national agreement," he supposedly told LaViers. "I can't modify it."

LaViers left Washington dejected. What he didn't know, as coal-industry watchdog Tom Bethel pointed out, is that the union had taken quite a different stance when its own company, West Kentucky Coal, had fallen behind on its Welfare Fund payments in 1959 and 1961. "Specifically the union had loaned the company almost $1 million to maintain royalty payments," Bethel writes. "The money came out of the union's National Bank of Washington, went through UMW headquarters, and on to West Kentucky Coal before making its way back to the National Bank of Washington in the form of Welfare Fund payments. The loan was never repaid. The national agreement to which Kennedy considered himself morally bound had not prevented his union from robbing Peter to pay Paul when circumstances called for it."

On March 5, 1962, union picket lines went up around South East's three mines. At almost exactly the same time, Consol stopped buying the company's coal for resale—but not, it claimed, because of the union contract's protective wage clause.

Consol doubted the legality of the clause and didn't pay any attention to it, George Love later said. In his own special brand of corporate doublethink, he testified that Consol had stopped buying the high-quality coal South East produced because it suddenly couldn't find any market for it. Besides, he said, he felt South East could do better by setting up its own sales agency. Indeed, the National Labor Relations Board did eventually declare the protective wage clause illegal. But the facts are that Consol had found plenty of markets for LaViers' coal between 1960 and the time South

East severed its UMW ties. During this period it sold a total of 403,443 tons of South East coal. After March, 1962, it didn't sell an ounce.

The history of the LaViers' coal company was one of constant conflict and struggle for the next five years. Picket lines with from 4 to 400 union members frequently surrounded their mines. Few dared cross them, for picket lines are regarded as sacred in the coalfields. Anyone who crosses one is automatically labeled a "scab." Those who did cross "were pretty desperate for work, they needed money real bad," according to Harry LaViers, Jr. Few had experience in a modern mine. "We had to start and train these people from scratch to operate rather complex pieces of machinery . . . it was a very slow process," he said. "In addition, even though we would get them trained, they would get scared and leave; they didn't stay too long."

Production, of course, dropped drastically for two years, but it returned to near-normal levels by 1964 and 1965. In the interim, South East continued to operate in the red as many would-be customers shied away from it in fear that the company might suddenly fold. To compete, the LaViers cut prices, adding further to their losses.

Other small coal companies faced the same situation as the arrangement tightened. But not Consol. Its net profits after taxes rose from just over $19 million in 1960 to an all-time high of more than $41 million in 1965.

The Second Pitch

In early 1965, just when better days appeared on the horizon, Harry LaViers, Sr., again went to Washington to talk to the UMW. At these meetings, George Titler, who later became the union vice-president, warned LaViers that the union's 1966 contract talks were underway. South East, he allegedly said, "is a thorn in our side and something has got to be done about it."

When LaViers returned home, he found new picket lines around his mines. This time, the strike was less effective. In May almost half of the company's employees were still on the job. The company had miraculously survived. In 1966 it filed suit charging that Consol and the UMW had conspired to drive it out of business in direct violation of the Sherman Anti-Trust Act.

"We didn't think big labor and big management should be able to sit down and set the terms for the whole industry. We didn't think anyone had the right to mark us for elimination," Harry LaViers, Jr., told me one morning in his sparse office in Irvine, Kentucky. "I felt I had the perfect right to stay in eastern Kentucky where I was born and my mother's family has lived since the 1700's."

The case came to trial in a U.S. District Court in Lexington, Kentucky, in October, 1968. After four weeks of testimony, the jurors retired to their chambers. A short while later they asked for an adding machine. Within four more hours, the jury announced it had found Consol and UMW guilty and assessed them damages totaling $7.2 million, plus attorney fees. It was the first time in U.S. history that a jury had found big management and big labor guilty of making a deal to dominate an entire industry.

South East Coal is fortunate. It survived. Two-thirds of all the Kentucky mines, employing roughly three-fourths of Kentucky's miners, didn't survive. They didn't have the resources or the persistence to fight back. They became the innocent victims of a cynical alliance between the highest levels of big labor and big management. The "arrangement" replaced men with machines. It replaced the mines where the men worked with a small network of high-yielding big mines owned by rich corporations based outside the region, and with dozens of destructive nonunion strip mines and marginal deep mines that often pay scandalously low wages and operate under shoddy safety conditions. The miners' and small mine operators' losses will never be recovered.

6

Tale of Two Miners

The "arrangement" changed coalcamp life forever. Thousands of miners, realizing the inevitable, took a last look at the crackerbox houses the coal companies had built decades before, packed their children and possessions into the family car, and headed north for Chicago or Detroit, Cleveland or Cincinnati. Others waited, not understanding what had happened, gathering each morning at the camp post office, hoping for the mine to reopen, and eventually succumbing to the welfare rolls.

Some fought back, vowing to remain at work doing the only thing they knew how to do. This chapter is about two of them: Darwin Clevinger and LeRoy Fields. Both men were loyal members of the UMW. Both stayed because their mines didn't shut down when others did. And both brought up their sons and daughters to stay away from the mines. A dozen years ago their views about the union and coal mining would have been almost identical. Today, largely because of the "arrangement" and the policies of the UMW, they are vastly different.

Darwin Clevinger

Clevinger was lounging in a colonial-style armchair as the rain beat down around his house off Marrowbone Creek in Wolf Pit, Kentucky. With his fingernails clean and his black hair slicked back like that of a leading man in a 1948 movie, he didn't look like a coal miner. He wore a freshly starched gray workshirt.

"I enjoy working in the mines," he said. "Miners are good people. You feel awful close together because it hurts real bad when one of your buddies gets killed. There's something about the mines. After a man works awhile in them he gets to like the work, and he doesn't want to do anything else. It grows on you."

Clevinger is 48. He is among the elite of Kentucky miners —a union man who has worked without major layoffs or injury for all of his 28 years in the mines, one of the working men the "arrangement" benefited. Mining has been good to him. He owns two cars, both Chevrolets, and a recently re-modeled house. His living-room walls are wood-paneled, and there is a plush carpet on the floor. He works in what he considers a "safe mine" and expects to earn up to $10,000 this year. In addition, the UMW Health and Welfare Fund guarantees him free hospital and medical care plus a $150 monthly pension when he reaches 55.

Clevinger's wife, Reble, an attractive brunette with large eyes, has never worked since they were married. She gets up with Darwin each day at 6:00 A.M., fills a thermos with hot coffee, and packs sandwiches, a piece of cake, a small can of fruit and a bar of chocolate into a lunch pail. "The average coal miner is a big eater," she says. After a breakfast of fried eggs, toast and bacon, Darwin leaves for Republic Steel's Rock Creek mine. It is a 20-minute ride across the Big Sandy River and south on U.S. 23. At the company bathhouse he puts on a pair of hardtoe shoes and his safety helmet (a miner's version of a hardhat) and slips out of his streetclothes into a pair of Washington Dee Cee overalls. By 8:00 A.M., he is "on the hill" at the driftmouth, or entrance to the mine, ready to board a "mantrip," or shuttle car, which will take him to where he and six other men work, a mile and a half underground. They arrive there at 8:20, check their machinery and start to work 15 minutes later. They continue until 3:30 P.M., with only one 30-minute break for lunch. There are no coffee breaks in coal mines.

The routine is the same throughout the day. A monstrous 30-ton machine, called a "continuous miner," grinds at the face of the coal, tearing it from the seam and preparing it for a series of conveyor belts that will carry it out of the mine. Clevinger runs a loading machine about ten feet behind the continuous miner. "It's hard work," he says. "There isn't an easy job in a coal mine. You're dirty from the time you put your clothes on."

At the end of the day, he is tired. He seldom does much more than watch television or work in the yard during the evenings, except on Friday when he drives to Pikeville, 20 miles away, for an Odd Fellows meeting. On Sunday there is church at Wolf Pit Baptist, and every other week a meeting of UMW Local 845 in the afternoon.

Clevinger is vice-president of local 845, and the union is important to him. He lights his filter-tip cigarettes with a "Tony Boyle" Zippo lighter given to him at the 1968 union convention in Denver. And he talks about how the union has made the difference between big money and little money for him. (The union wage scale was $37 a day in 1971.) The big money, he says, shows up in the houses union members own and the clothes their children wear to school. A union man can live comfortably in poverty-scarred areas like Pike County, Kentucky. His medical bills and pension are taken care of by the UMW Health and Welfare Fund. Union protection makes his mine safer.

"A nonunion man's got nothing to look forward to," he adds.

A nonunion miner can't afford a decent place to live. Wages are low (sometimes just $12 for an eight-hour day). Often they are drawn in "cash-in-advance" loans so that when payday finally comes checks are small, and the miner is continually in debt to the company that employs him.

"You never did hear of cash-in-advance at a union mine," Clevinger said in a soft, matter-of-fact drawl. "The union's good for the miner. It's made it so I could educate my children pretty well. What I couldn't of done any other way.

"I educated them not to be miners," he said. " 'Druther they stayed away from the mines." His oldest son, 28-year-old Gary, is a barber in Ohio. Terry, 21, is a senior at Morehead, Kentucky, State University, majoring in business management. His daughter Kitty, 17, is a senior at nearby Millard High School, and he would prefer that she not marry a miner.

The evening had grown late. The rain outside Clevinger's comfortable living room had turned to a light drizzle. His wife and daughter were at a basketball game at the high school. Soon they'd be home, and he would turn in for the night.

Yes, he was aware of the charges of corruption made against the UMW, and he knew that union membership in his home county, the second-largest coal producing county in the nation, had dwindled to less than one-third of what it once was. The UMW could use some improvement, he said. Something should be done for widows and disabled miners. Vacations (he gets 3 weeks after 28 years at the same mine) and sickday benefits (there are none) could be better.

But after a long pause, he added:

"The union is sound. Tony Boyle done a wonderful job for the coal miner."

LeRoy Fields

A warped plank footbridge over Thorton Creek leads to LeRoy Fields' place. The creek is only a tiny trickle that winds its way down the hollow toward the Cumberland River. It's distinguished by the dozens of empty Van Camp pork and beans cans that litter its bed. LeRoy Fields' place has red tar-paper siding. It's distinguished by the old wringer washing machine on the porch. "When the missus washes," he says, "it shakes like the world's going to end."

There wasn't any washing going on this December day. It was 10:30 A.M., and Fields was embarrassed that he was still eating breakfast. "We're both sick, don't you know," said his wife, a gentle matronly woman whose gray hair was pulled back in a bun. "Don't you know we just can't get started."

Fields was eating cornbread and gravy. He is a proud, stubby man of 65. He looks older, mostly because he went into the mines when he was 14 and stayed 46 years. His wife bore him 11 children whose pictures, taken in high-school graduation dresses and army and navy uniforms, adorn the pale green walls of the living room and the ledge above the fireplace in the Fields' bedroom.

"I saw some bad times," Fields said. "In Hoover's day we made just $1.76 for 12 hours work, and me with a big family.

If I hadn't growed it [food] out of the ground, we'd have starved. I hoed at it many a night with just the light from my carbide lamp. People laid down in the road in them days and starved to death. My sister boiled grass and chewed weeds to make it."

Fields is a preacher in the Holiness, or Church of God, faith, and he doesn't like to speak ill of his fellow man. "I don't even want to think wrong about anyone," he says. But because he is a preacher, and because he feels so very strongly about the subject, it doesn't take him long to warm up into an evangelistic fervor over the UMW.

"I fought so much and cried and prayed for that union. And then I got flat turned out," he said. "Someone, somewhere sold out. They sold me and all the miners around here out."

Fields feels amply qualified to speak on the subject. He is one of tens of thousands of miners deserted by the UMW. He joined the union as a charter member of his local in 1933 when the union first organized Letcher County, Kentucky, and he served as local vice-president for more than two decades.

"I marched around Crummies Creek [the scene of several bloody shootouts during UMW organizing drives] when they told you, 'You go over there and you won't come back,'" he recalled. "I went because I thought the union was holding up for the right thing, better wages and such. I was a minister so I never went to jail. I just stayed in the picket lines and prayed for everybody."

Fields coughed a loud tubercular cough and continued. "I sweated out all those strikes with that big family. That's not easy. That's what irks me. We stayed out for their promise that we'd be taken care of. Then we get in old age and they sit on a man's stomach. I've laid and cried about this."

He moved slowly out of the kitchen into the living room, a small, tidy room with a linoleum floor. The room, along with most of the house, had been remodeled with an FHA loan two years before, a loan that takes $48 a month out of his Social Security check. A black wrought-iron plaque was hung above the couch. It said:

Bless
This House
Oh Lord
Pray, Make It
Safe By Night.

Fields' disillusionment with the UMW began at a night meeting in 1962. Like thousands of other loyal union members, he worked in a small mine, owned by Big Three Coal Company, at the time. For years, Big Three Coal, and hundreds of companies like it, had not kept up with its 40-cents-per-ton royalty payment to the UMW Health and Welfare Fund. It was only one of many companies with sweetheart arrangements; with a declining coal market, many of the companies simply couldn't afford the levy. The union blinked, allowing the payments to lapse, but it did not tell local union members about the arrangement. Then, in 1962, the union abruptly announced it would no longer allow companies to fail to pay the levy. Miners throughout eastern Kentucky went on strike, attempting to force the beleaguered coal companies to make the fund payments. As Fields recalled it, the strike had lasted three weeks when UMW field representative Joe Davis gathered local officers.

"Davis told us, 'Go back, we can't carry you no longer on strike benefits,'" Fields reminisced. "'We can't negotiate with you out of the mines,' he said. 'LeRoy, take them back to work and we'll fix it.' He hammered his fist on the table and said, 'We will do it.' "

Davis didn't "fix it." The moment Fields and the other miners went back to work, the Big Three Coal Company mine became a nonunion mine, and all the miners automatically became "scabs." Within a month, the UMW revoked Fields' medical card, which provided him free medical care, and refused to take his dues payments. Fields kept working. "What could a man do," he said. "I still had three children at home to feed. Weren't no other jobs nowhere in these parts."

He is still baffled by exactly what happened and why—particularly since the union has now rejected his application for a retirement pension.

"I just can't imagine how people you held so much confidence in could do you so bad," he said. His words were choked with emotion. "They betrayed Jesus for 30 pieces of silver. Don't you know some leaders will sell you out for a piece of silver."

His eyes dropped to the floor and he shook his head. "Somebody got some silver," he said. "I got nothing. Not even thanks. All this whole country been done this way."

7

The Fund

The two great ironies in the recent history of the United Mine Workers union are men like Curtis Collier and the UMW Health and Welfare Fund.

Their stories are interlocking.

The fund's irony lies in the fact that a quarter-century after it was created as a living monument to John L. Lewis it is remembered more for the bitterness it has caused than for the goodwill and security it offers.

Curtis Collier's irony is more personal. It lies in his loyalty to the union—and in his legs. "Never was a more loyal union man," he boasts. "The UMW, it was the greatest thing that ever happened to this here country."

Collier's legs, however, indicate the union has not returned the same devotion. He showed them to me one autumn day as we sat beside the grocery store his son runs on

Franks Creek in Eolia, Kentucky. "No man knows what I've had to go through," he said, hiking up his right pants leg. "Sometimes I think I'd rather of died on the job than be the way I am."

Collier, a rotund little man with a pencil-thin mustache, was chewing Mail Pouch tobacco. He spat a juicy brown wad of it into a rusty coffee can and peeled off a green wool sock, exposing a deep, ugly scar that ran six inches down his lower leg to a large cavity where doctors had removed an ankle joint 30 years before. His left leg was in worse shape. An artificial limb made of plastic and wood grown yellow with age, it was strapped to a stump four inches above the knee.

Both legs were crushed in 1939 when a six-ton motor, a shuttle car used to transport coal underground, pinned him against a rail. Within a year, he was back on the job. He stayed until 1949, often working two eight-hour shifts back-to-back to support his wife and three growing children. When he left it was only on doctors' orders.

The UMW Health and Welfare Fund was new and full of promises in those days. Collier and half a million other miners had struck three times in two years to see it become a reality. He thought it would take care of him. The fund had given him a medical card entitling him to free doctor and hospital care, and pledging pensions and disability payments. "I wasn't exactly a poor man," Collier recalled. "I had saved while I was working. I figured with some help from the union me and the little lady could get by."

He learned otherwise soon. The first blow came in January, 1954, when fund trustees canceled the free medical benefits and disability payments ($30 a month for each miner and $10 for each dependent) of Collier and some 30,000 other permanently injured union members. In a drastic policy reversal, the trustees contended maimed miners were the responsibility of state and federal governments. This left Collier and thousands like him out in the cold. The only assistance he could qualify for was disability payments under Social Security, which as late as 1970 totaled only $118.50 a month. The second blow came in 1965 when the UMW rejected his application for a union pension. He was told eligibility rules had changed since he left the mines. Collier felt he had earned the pension. He joined the union during the bloody organizing days of the 1930's and stuck with it, often picketing under the muzzles of company rifles. When he didn't get the pension, he felt betrayed.

"I've been wronged," he said, pushing his black baseball cap back on his head. "Those trustees up there destroyed my life."

He paused, then hobbled toward the tiny ripple of water that is Franks Creek. His artificial leg made a slushing sound like a plumber's plunger as he walked. He mumbled that his health had been failing for a year. He had suffered a stroke and a heart attack. He had high blood pressure, and his legs bothered him. Often he'd wake up at night with a gripping chill that would go away only after he submerged his body in the bathtub.

"Just the other day the doc he told me, 'Curt, you're apt to die at any moment just like that.' Suspect everyone's apt to go sometime. But I love to live—I love life.

"I've tried to live right," Collier said. "I didn't want to have anyone give me anything I didn't earn. I just wanted justice."

Back When

No one anticipated such future bitterness on September 2, 1948, when John L. Lewis presented the fund's first $100 pension check to Horace Michael Ainscough, a 62-year-old miner from Rock Springs, Wyoming. "God bless the day John L. Lewis was born," Ainscough said as he accepted the check.

Lewis nodded his bushy mane and said something impressive in a ceremonial flourish. It was an important day for him. The fund was his brainchild. He conceived of it as a plan to give security to miners and their families whose lives had long been scarred by the nation's most dangerous occupation. In the 35 years prior to 1945, 2 million men were maimed in mine accidents. Almost 69,000 of them were killed, many of them buried alive in dark, lonely catacombs far underground. Those who lived were left with twisted backs, lost limbs, paralyzed bodies and burned flesh. To add to their misery, medical standards in the Appalachian region were primitive to the point of being a national disgrace, according to the Boone Report, the result of a 1946 presidential fact-finding mission.

It was Lewis' theory that consumers and coal companies, who were responsible for this human ruin, should bear the cost of the fund. Financing would be tied to production on a pay-as-you-go basis with a levy on every ton of coal produced.

His union in those days was tough and militant. In the words of the *Washington Evening Star*, " . . . the United Mine workers spoke with a voice of thunder. And when they spoke the nation listened—attentively." Three times between 1946 and 1948 miners followed Lewis out of the pits to see his welfare plan become a reality. The strikes reduced the nation's coal supply to dangerously low levels and earned for Lewis the title of "Public Enemy No. One" in much of the press. Federal judges repeatedly hauled him into court. On one occasion, a judge fined him $10,000 and the union

$350,000; on another he was fined $20,000 and the union $1.4 million.

But the strikes and the fines paid fat dividends. In 1946, President Truman seized the nation's mines during a lengthy walkout and directed the Secretary of the Interior Julius A. Krug to negotiate a contract with the UMW. Eight days later, a Krug-Lewis agreement was signed in the White House providing for a "welfare and retirement fund to be financed by payments into the fund for operating managers of 5 cents per ton on each ton of coal produced for use or sale." Two years later the royalty was raised to 20 cents per ton. (It rose to 30 cents in 1950 and to 40 cents in 1952, where it stayed until 1971 when it was hiked to 80 cents.)

Lewis's "great dream" had become a reality. By the late 1940's, the fund offered a "womb-to-tomb" welfare program to miners, free of cost. It was the collective bargaining triumph of the decade, a program unmatched by that of most other labor unions: free medical and hospital care for working miners, $100 monthly pensions for those over 60, medical care and cash benefits for the disabled, and $1,000 funeral checks for widows. "Here in one sweep," Saul Alinski wrote in his biography of Lewis, "he [Lewis] wrestled for his half-million miners that complete security that suddenly made life free from fear and filled with all the essentials for the pursuit of happiness."

Alinski's words were written in 1949, the same year Curtis Collier left the mines. Today, they have a hollow ring in Appalachia. In the intervening years, the fund had received $3.1 billion in royalties and each year dispensed pensions and medical care to about 252,000 miners and their families. It had revolutionized medical standards in much of the region. For those miners able to qualify for its benefits, it was a godsend. It paid for treatment of their broken backs and limbs and for delivery of their babies; it gave them pensions in their old age.

But thousands of miners, perhaps a majority of those working in 1949, were without benefits. For them, the fund is better known for what it hasn't done than for what it has. Many feel it has simply deserted Appalachia. They have good cause for concern. In the early 1960's, the fund sold the ten ultramodern hospitals it had built for miners. Untold thousands—nobody knows exactly how many—of disabled miners, widows and working miners have been arbitrarily denied benefits without hearing or recourse. For those able to stay eligible, pension payments have fluctuated continually, dropping as low as $75 a month at one point.

In the meantime, the fund's shortcomings have begun to catch up with it. Senate investigators and the U.S. Solicitor General have found that political manipulation and incredible mismanagement now threaten the fund's very solvency and jeopardize payments to its unsuspecting future beneficiaries. In an even harsher indictment of fund practices, a federal judge has ordered broad reforms in its management after finding UMW leaders guilty of a conspiracy designed to enrich the union and the union-owned National Bank of Washington at the expense of union members and beneficiaries of the fund.

Pensions for Profit and Political Gain

When the Health and Welfare Fund comes under fire, as it has so often in recent years, members of the UMW hierarchy make much ado about how they'd like to straighten it out, but they have no control over it. Technically, they're right. On paper, the fund is independent of the union, as required by Taft-Hartley-Act regulations. It has separate offices one block from the cathedral-like union headquarters and a 325-member staff of its own.

In reality, however, the fund is the union's most lucrative operation and is closely tied to the union administration, by which it can be used as a convenient vehicle for profit and political gain. Miners wishing to apply for pensions, for instance, must do so through their local unions and, to remain eligible to receive them, must pay $1.25 monthly dues—a bonanza that some have compared to extortion and that nets the union treasury $1 million a year. Such policies are made by the three trustees who direct fund affairs: one representing the union, one management, and one neutral interests. Until a federal judge ordered him to vacate the post June 30, 1971, the union's trustee was none other than W. Anthony Boyle, the UMW president, or "mine chieftain" as the UMW *Journal* affectionately calls him. Although he admitted, "When I go over there as a trustee I'm strictly a novice," Boyle was also chairman of the fund and thus its chief executive officer.

Until the same ruling, the "neutral" trustee and director of the fund since 1948 had been Miss Josephine Roche, an 84-year-old spinster who was a longtime intimate of John L. Lewis. An articulate grandmotherly figure, Miss Roche helped Lewis design the fund and probably knows more about its operations than anyone else. She has been close to the union ever since 1928, when the Rocky Mountain Fuel Company, which she inherited, became the first coal company west of the Mississippi to sign a union contract. The relationship has proved to be highly profitable for Miss Roche. She collects an annual salary of $60,000, $10,000 more than the union pays Boyle. In addition, she has indirectly benefited from a $1.4-million loan Lew-Mur-Ken, an unusual UMW-owned holding company, received from the union treasury and never repaid. Lew-Mur-Ken apparently used much of the $1.4 million to buy a 30 percent ownership in the Rocky Mountain Fuel Company—the same year it went bankrupt.

The third member of the fund triumvirate is C. W. Davis, who became trustee because one of his predecessors as management representative, George Judy, allowed Boyle to ramrod through a 30-percent pension increase in a blatant show of union domination of the fund. The coup ultimately cost Judy his job as chairman of the Bituminous Coal Operators Association and won Boyle another four-year term as UMW president. It came during Boyle's frantic campaign for reelection in 1969 and only 13 days after John L. Lewis's death. Boyle had just been named to take Lewis's seat as fund trustee when he called Judy and informed him he wanted a meeting within 20 hours. When Judy arrived at UMW headquarters, the union president said he wanted to increase the pensions of 70,000 miners from $115 to $150 a month. Judy, who had been appointed a trustee just three weeks before and, like Boyle, knew little about the fund's financial condition, balked at first. He testified before a Senate subcommittee that Thomas Ryan, the fund comptroller, cautioned that the hike would cost $30 million a year and cut into vital fund reserves. Boyle put him at ease. "It doesn't make too much difference whether you vote for it or not, this thing is going to pass," Judy recalled the union president saying. "I've got Josephine Roche here in my pocket, a proxy."

This was untrue. Miss Roche, who was hospitalized with a hip injury and couldn't attend the meeting, opposed the increase. She told Senate investigators that the action "reaches directly into the possibility of other benefits having to be curtailed." But this was ten months later—long after Boyle and Judy had approved the increase and sent word of it to pensioners with a note signed "W. A. Boyle, Trustee," long after pensioners had given Boyle a nine-to-one edge in balloting for the union presidency and put him in office for four more years.

No one quarreled with the need for the increase. Pensioners hadn't had a raise in their monthly allotments for four years, and the checks had grown only $15 a month since Horace Ainscough received the first one 21 years before. Living costs had more than doubled in the meantime. However, Boyle's methods and the fund's obvious inability to absorb the increase brought storms of protest. When coal operators learned of it, they corraled Judy. They found to their amazement that although Judy had committed them to the increase, no one could say precisely how much it would cost. For one thing, none of the operators knew how many miners were eligible for pensions. Moreover, no actuarial study of the pension fund had been made since 1948.

The operators, representing such industrial giants as the Consolidation Coal Company, were astounded by the lack of such elementary data and sound business practice. An inquiry by a Senate labor subcommittee into fund operations drew the same looks of puzzlement from senators. At one point Boyle could not even tell them exactly how many members his union had. At another, subcommittee chairman Senator Harrison Williams scolded Boyle for, in effect, buying the pension vote. At Williams' request, the General Accounting Office made an intensive study of the fund and found that it would become insolvent by 1973 unless some changes were made. "It is our opinion that the $35 a month increase in pension benefits should not have been made without definite arrangements for obtaining additional income," the GAO report concluded.

The fund's financial records and its relationship with the National Bank of Washington have also raised eyebrows and produced a stern scolding from a federal judge. When first asked about them, Boyle hesitated to supply senators with records of the fund's financial wheelings and dealings, claiming that their publication might "operate to the detriment of the trust fund." What he was apparently attempting to conceal was the fund's incredible investment record and the already widely publicized fact that for years it had kept from $20 to $100 million in non-interest-drawing checking accounts in the National Bank of Washington. The accounts cost the fund up to $5 million a year in lost interest, or roughly enough for some 3,100 miner pensions.

Boyle and other fund spokesmen testified before the Senate labor subcommittee that deposits were down to $33.8 million in April, 1970. The accounts would be continued, they said, for "emergency purposes," or what one senator described as "reasons of nervousness." One year later, a federal judge ordered the fund to remove the deposits and place them in a bank not connected with the union or the coal industry.

The reason for the order lies in the ownership of the bank. The union controls 74 percent of its stock. Until recently, Boyle, UMW counsel Edward Carey and fund comptroller Thomas Ryan sat on the bank's board of directors, along with such dignitaries as Clark Clifford, former Secretary of Defense, and True Davis, president of the bank and a former Assistant Secretary of the Treasury. The non-interest accounts were, in effect, a giant windfall to the bank. They gave it free money—from $10 million to over $25 million over one five-year period—to invest for its own profit.

As the largest stockholder, the union in turn reaped benefits in terms of higher dividends that flowed into its coffers for dispersal at the wish of the UMW hierarchy.

These dividends totaled $1.5 million in 1969. Union officers have benefited from the special relationship with the bank in other ways, too. Although bank president Davis has denied any knowledge of it and has stated he feels it to be bad bank policy, several union officials, including a son of UMW secretary-treasurer John Owens, have received loans from the bank.

There is no such convenient explanation for the fund's common stock portfolio. Fund trustees and comptroller Thomas Ryan have purchased some $44 million worth of common stock in 17 electric-utility companies over the years. They have done so without competent professional advice, relying instead on what Ryan has described as "just a real, general, intensive knowledge and experience over a period of 25 to 30 years in working in business and finance." Ryan collects a $50,000 annual salary, but his experience hasn't proven all that valuable to the stock portfolio. While everyone else was getting rich from the stock market in the middle 1960's, the fund's portfolio showed a paper loss of $5 million, which Senator Clairborne Pell has said "is pretty difficult to achieve."

Miners have become accustomed to such abuse. While Miss Roche and the union hierarchy have played with the fund for profit and political gain, thousands of miners have been arbitrarily cut off from its benefits and left to perish on the slag heaps of sickness, poverty and old age. While the full-time employees of the fund have enjoyed average annual salaries of $12,606, miners who have remained eligible for fund benefits have never seen their monthly pension checks rise above $150. They have had little recourse. The fund's policy-making and administration are entirely in the hands of the three trustees. As the fund's annual report puts it, all benefits "are subject to termination, revision, or amendment by the trustees in their discretion at any time."

The trustees have used this discretion frequently—to the detriment of thousands of miners. In 1954, for instance, they abruptly eliminated the small cash benefit checks paid to 30,000 disabled miners (including Curtis Collier), even though three-fourths of those miners had no other source of income and about 70 percent were totally disabled. Later that same year, 24,000 widows, 90 percent of them said to be "aged," and their children lost their cash benefits. Six years later, free medical benefits were taken away from those among the 54,000 who had been able to retain them as well as from untold thousands of union members who had been put out of work by union-endorsed mechanization and a paralyzing recession in the coalfields.

This latter cutback struck harder than any of the previous cuts. Even today much of the bitterness about the fund dates back to "that day in 1960 when they took my medical card." Protest rallies were called in Kentucky and Pennsylvania, and wildcat strikes shut down half a dozen mines in West Virginia. Yet the short-lived rebellion was almost forgotten by 1962, when the fund made another cutback and thousands more miners were deprived not only of union benefits but of union membership as well. The most frustrating rule change of all took place in 1965, when the trustees announced that younger miners—and those older ones still working in union mines—would no longer have to meet the rigid pension requirements drawn up in 1953. The 1953 rule change had stated that to qualify for a pension a miner must have worked 20 of the last 30 years in a mine. Prior to that time, and after 1965, miners could count any time worked in the mines toward their 20-year total as long as other requirements were met. In the meantime, thousands of loyal union members had been systematically deprived of their pensions.

Fund spokesmen, of course, deny this. They say changes have always been dictated by finanical conditions and have been made in the interest of the most possible miners. Miss Roche, for instance, has said: "We have always advocated and worked and suffered intensively to try to get increases for pensions and every other benefit, but always observing the basic obligation that we must maintain the fiscal integrity of the fund. And on a pay-as-you-go basis we must not permit increases in outgo to exceed the income that is coming to us from royalties."

The Rejects

Not everyone agrees that the fund has done everything it could over the years, particularly the thousands who have been systematically deprived of its benefits. In the summer of 1970, a small band of them, known as the Disabled Miners of Southern West Virginia, decided to do something about it. They first approached district union officials in Beckley, West Virginia, requesting a meeting with UMW president Boyle to discuss medical benefits for disabled miners and widows.

When Boyle refused to meet them and district union leaders gave them no satisfaction, the miners and widows called a wildcat strike. The association's members, many of them crippled and deformed, set up picket lines across the southern West Virginia coalfields. Within a week, 14,000 miners were off their jobs and the strike had spread, shutting down dozens of mines across the state and in parts of Kentucky and Pennsylvania. The stoppage continued for more than a month at a time when electrical "brownouts" threatened much of the Eastern seaboard and utility companies complained of severe coal shortages.

A U.S. Senate subcommittee, which had been investigating fund operations for months, chose this time to hold a public hearing in Charleston, West Virginia. Three senators caught a late-afternoon jet out of Washington for the occasion. They would stay a few hours, then jet back to a full night's sleep far removed from the grim realities of the coalfields.

In the meantime, they sat attentively at the front of a wood-paneled courtroom on the fifth floor of the local federal building listening to how the UMW Health and Welfare Fund worked.

Those who would tell them about it, one widow and nine former miners with twisted bodies, faced them in the first two rows on the right. Among them were Willie Sadler, from Logan County, whose wife had been in a coma for 21 months and who had no way to pay the medical bills; Clarence J. Powers, who was only 40 but looked like he'd just stepped from the grave; Lewis Hess, from Delbarton in Mingo County, who said one of his legs had rotted off after a mine accident; his neighbor, Luther Justice, who didn't have any legs at all; and Mrs. Virginia Rothwell, a widow who worked at a YMCA for $1 an hour to support herself because she couldn't qualify for help from the union or the government.

Each had a story to tell about how the UMW Health and Welfare Fund had wronged them and their families. Each story seemed worse than the one before. One by one the nine miners and the widow hobbled or were wheeled to a microphone to have their words recorded in an obscure committee report that few people would ever read.

Luther Justice, the father of six, told how he had worked 21½ years in union mines before a runaway coal car ran over his legs, but couldn't get any help from the fund. "It's a bad life to live and not get paid for it," he said.

Mrs. Rothwell, a matronly-looking woman in a plaid cotton housedress, said her husband died in 1966 from a heart attack caused by black lung, which he had acquired during his 40 years as a UMW member and active coal miner. "Now I don't get anything," she said. "I'm not bitter to anyone—I'm making it, but it's hard."

Kelley Baisden, from Mingo County, was the final witness among the miners. A slight, skeleton-like figure, he said he was 45. He looked 30 years older. His cheeks were caverns, and when he breathed they puffed out as if he were blowing up a balloon. The sound of the air coming in and out could be heard throughout the room.

Baisden had been a miner 16 years, he said, until a slate fall severed a nerve in his back in 1957. His lungs went bad during his years in the mines, and now he also had a nervous disorder and kidney trouble. His lungs were the biggest problem, though. They made his breath short and caused him to make from 15 to 20 trips a year, many of them emergency ones, to the Appalachian Regional Hospital in Beckley, three hours' driving time from his home. "They tell me if I'm going to live any, in a couple years I'll need pure oxygen all the time," he said.

As he finished the sentence, Baisden gasped for breath. His friend Lew Hess brought him a portable respirator ("My breathing machine," he said later). Baisden coughed a deep, guttural cough. "That talking cuts my oxygen off," he said.

Baisden puffed into the respirator for several minutes before continuing. He said the Health and Welfare Fund had helped him greatly after his accident, but it abruptly cut his benefits in 1960. He had no health insurance and has found no one to insure him since. In the meantime, his medical bills continue to grow and have now reached more than $3,000. He has no way to pay them and little hope of ever being able to do so. His monthly income from Social Security and welfare checks totals $366. He has eight children.

What do you think about the welfare fund today? one senator asked.

"We just feel we've been pushed into the background and forgotten about," he said.

8

Death to the Insurgent

From the bottom of the hill, the three graves were barely visible, barely distinguishable from the big granite slabs around them. Closer, one saw the three red vigil lights and the fresh green boughs of Scotch pine. Beside the flickering light on the right lay the body of the young social-worker daughter. Next to her, the mother. And on the left, the father, the fiery coal miner who had challenged the leadership of the United Mine Workers union. There were no headstones to identify the three or tell of their tragic death. The pink burial cards in the caretaker's office did that. "Joseph Albert Yablonski, Age 59, R.D. 1, Clarksville, Pa.," the one for the father said. "Cause of Death: Shot, Murdered."

Mike Trbovitch, who mines coal at the Gateway mine in Carteirs, Pennsylvania, stared at the graves. "It's a helluva price to pay for a little democracy," he said. "It's just a waste of human life."

One year before, almost to the day, Trbovitch had watched the three caskets lowered into the ground. It had been a cold day, even for January, and a cruel wind had blown across the hill overlooking the Washington, Pennsylvania, cemetery. A blizzard had blanketed southwestern Pennsylvania a day before, and the three hearses from the Burkus Funeral Home had trouble making it up the hill.

The network television cameras and dozens of newsmen had been there that day, and about 800 mourners: a congressman, a few local politicians and some neighbors, but mostly coal miners, who had fought alongside Yablonski, and their wives. Trbovitch had been a pallbearer.

Now, a year later, we were alone. A warmer breeze blew off Highway 18, and big, soft flakes of snow blanketed the cemetery, making it look pure and innocent.

"I was sick that day. I'm still sick," Trbovitch said. There was nothing to add. We hung our heads. Then we walked down the hill.

The year had been a difficult one for Mike Trbovitch. His hair had turned gray. He had lost 10 pounds. And his wife worried about his safety.

"Three good people died because our government failed to enforce the law," he said. "To me it wasn't worth it."

The Yablonski murders had shocked the nation. The FBI combed four states for the killers, eventually gaining indictments of five men—including one minor union official. The Labor Department, which had repeatedly denied Yablonski's requests that it investigate the "reign of terror" in the union, suddenly deemed it necessary to send 217 agents into the field. They returned reports of massive irregularities in the reelection of Yablonski's opponent for the UMW leadership—incumbent President W. A. Boyle—and the department filed a suit seeking to overturn the balloting.

It all began in the Pan American Room of the Mayflower Hotel in Washington, D.C., one day late in May, 1969. Two young men blocked the entryway, carefully scrutinizing the credentials of newsmen who presented themselves. At just after 11:00 A.M., Joseph A. "Jock" Yablonski, a name unknown to most of those present, rose to announce he intended to do something no one had done successfully in more than 40 years—unseat the leadership of the UMW.

A stocky union official from Pennsylvania, Yablonski had unlikely credentials as a reformer. He had spent most of his life as a part of the corrupt and authoritarian union machine. He had risen to its highest councils. He had accepted its ways and rewards, including a salary and expense account that totaled almost $50,000 in 1968.

The press conference severed those ties. In a deep, rasping voice he charged the UMW leadership with massive corruption, "shocking ineptitude and passivity," nepotism and a "neglect of miners' needs and aspirations."

"I participated in and tolerated the deteriorating performance of this leadership, but with increasingly troubled conscience," he declared. "I will be no longer be beholden to the past."

The UMW leadership was no stranger to criticism. It had been a daily fact of life for much of the union's 79-year history. Coal operators had long labeled its organizers "communists" and its wage demands "inflationary and ruinous."

In recent years, the attacks had been renewed. In Washington, consumer crusader Ralph Nader charged that the union had abdicated its role as the only force strong enough to combat political and economic corruption in Appalachia. It had declined, he said, into "a clique, dividing the spoils of union dues among narrow, callous leadership and local retainers."

Few of the accusations filtered through the granite fortress in Washington that houses the union's headquarters. The reformers, Tony Boyle would gripe in his office with the high ceiling and paneled walls, were pesky, ill-informed "outsiders" who wanted to "take over the greatest union in the world."

Yablonski was a different matter. He was an insider, a union loyalist for 36 years. He knew how the union worked, its wheelings and dealings and where the skeletons were buried. His ties with the rank and file were established. He would be harder to discredit, harder to intimidate.

The effort to deal with Yablonski would, of course, surely come. No one knew this better than Jock Yablonski himself. From the start, he said it would be an uphill battle, rife with danger. "They'll use every dollar they're able to spend, they'll use the full time of every payroller," he told newsmen at the Mayflower Hotel. The doors were guarded to keep out UMW spies. "I am not naive enough to think there won't be much difficulty. I know the ends to which they'll go."

Later, he confided to intimates that he could be murdered for what he had done that day. One month later, a karate chop across the neck knocked him unconscious following a rally in Springfield, Illinois.

The Candidates

The incumbent and the insurgent had striking similarities. Both were short and bald. Boyle's hair ended almost exactly in the middle of his head. Yablonski's inched slightly farther forward toward his sloping forehead. Both became miners as teen-agers: Yablonski at 15, Boyle at 16. Both their fathers died as a result of work in the mines. Both were ambitious and rose rapidly through union ranks during the great organization drives of the 1930's and early 1940's. Both developed expensive tastes and a knack for huge expense accounts. And both modeled their oratorical style after that of John L. Lewis.

Boyle's roots were in the western coalfields of Montana. Yablonski's were in the rolling hills of southwestern Pennsylvania, where he raised his family in the small (population 1,200) town of Clarksville. His wife, Margaret, was an amateur playwright. He first entered the mines in the grimy coaltown of California, Pennsylvania, as a high-school dropout. He made his first move for union office when only 24 and was elected president of a 1,200-man local. Eight years later he defeated an incumbent backed by dissident anti-Lewis forces to win a seat on the prestigious International Executive Board, a post he held for the next 27 years.

Boyle built an early reputation for doing "John L.'s dirty work." Yablonski's reputation was one for being a tough negotiator and a wheeler-dealer adept at grabbing plums for the union. "When Jock went in on a grievance, he won it for the miners," one associate recalls. "That's the kind of guy he was. He didn't take any bullshit."

The two union leaders were never close friends. Privately, Yablonski would say he had chafed under Boyle's presidency for years. Publicly, he took a different stance, often lionizing Boyle before crowds of miners. One of his duties was to introduce the UMW president at union gatherings. He did it well—too well, according to many, heaping lavish praise on his superior. Never did he mention the massive wrongdoings he later attacked. ("If you expect to stay, this is what you have to do," he once said.) But his flattery of Boyle made his late change-about suspect. As West Virginia miner Harry Patrick put it, "He'd been part and parcel of that gang since the year one."

Round One

The campaign developed into one of the most bitter in the history of the American labor movement. Tony Boyle started it by firing Yablonski from a job he had given him a month before. Yablonski, he said, wasn't "carrying out the policies of the international organization."

No, he added later, it didn't have anything to do with the Yablonski declaration of candidacy six days before. Yablonski simply was being ordered to Pittsburgh for "reassignment" because he hadn't shown enough interest in the job as acting director of the Labor's NonPartisan League, the union's lobbying arm.

Yablonski's attorney, Joseph L. Rauh, Jr., sued for his clients' reinstatement. Six weeks later a federal judge ordered that the challenger be given his job back. But more important than the decision, or the firing itself, was the pattern of vindictiveness it set for the duration of the campaign. Four times in the next seven months the Yablonski camp was forced into federal courts to secure for itself basic rights that are taken for granted in most elections and supposedly guaranteed by federal law. Rauh, a well-known Washington civil-rights attorney, won valuable concessions in all the cases, but not before critical campaign days were wasted over such elementary issues as keeping Boyle forces from using the UMW *Journal* as a propaganda tool.

On six other occasions, Rauh appealed to the Department of Labor for intervention, documenting dozens of specific allegations of intimidation, misuse of union funds and the union's "reign of terror." "This union is a private government—like the Mafia," he said later. "It operates above the law."

To each request, the Labor Department answered, "No,"

although the Landrum-Griffin Act directs it to supervise union elections. It is a "long standing policy," then Secretary of Labor George P. Shultz said repeatedly, not to "investigate and publicize the activities of one faction in an election in order to assist the campaign of the other."

John L. Lewis's death June 11, 1969, cleared the way for Boyle's most blatant power play. Although he had officially retired as union president nine years before, Lewis had retained a $35,000-a-year job as one of the three directors of the UMW Health and Welfare Fund. Immediately after his death, the International Executive Board named Boyle as his replacement. The following day, as we have seen, Boyle ramrodded through a 30 percent (from $115 to $150 a month) increase in the pensions paid to 70,000 retired miners, who more than coincidentally would make up a majority in the union election six months away. He called the meeting at which the hike was approved on 20 hours' notice, and the only other trustee to attend knew nothing of the plans for the increase until he arrived at UMW headquarters. Indeed, no one had figured out how to pay for the increase. Later, the U.S. General Accounting Office would find the hasty action had endangered the solvency of the entire pension fund; a federal court would order Boyle to give up his post as a fund trustee; and U.S. Senator Harrison Williams would charge that Boyle, in effect, had bought the union election. But this all occurred months *after* Boyle had won reelection to another four-year term—with the help of nine out of every ten pensioner votes.

Round Two

The campaign was a lonely one for Yablonski. Sometimes at the urging of his supporters he'd journey into the coalfields to meet miners; other times he wouldn't. When he did, the crowds often were small. Some were intimidated by union payrollers who stationed themselves outside meeting halls compiling lists of miners who went in. Others suspected Yablonski's past and motives. Even his running mate, Elmer Brown, a disabled miner from Delbarton, West Virginia, had his doubts about the candidate's sincerity.

Nevertheless, by mid-August Yablonski had scored a major breakthrough. He had won the nomination of 96 of the union's 1,400 local unions—almost twice the number needed to gain a spot on the December ballot. This had been no easy matter. Every union has dozens of payrollers eager to "volunteer" their time to support the incumbent responsible for their jobs. According to Labor Department records, the UMW had thoughtfully added 69 new faces to their payroll since the first of the year. Almost half of them were in Yablonski's home district, where voting was expected to be close. Dozens more found temporary employment with the union.

In Pennsylvania, local union officers were hired as "organizers" for six-week periods. When they arrived at their organizing sites, however, they found little to do but lounge in their motels, collect $75-a-day salaries and listen to Boyle propagandists. Some went fishing. One took the opportunity to vacation in Canada. He collected $2,409 for his nonwork and continued to support Yablonski. "Easiest money I ever made," he told Senate investigators.

Payoffs were less subtle in other areas, according to sworn testimony. Frank Sablonsky, a former district union official, told of being assigned to a special team to visit miners and retired union members during the nomination period. "The mission was that we would give them money for those people to go along with the nomination of Tony Boyle," he said. He witnessed payoffs of from $20 to $30 per person.

The stakes were higher in some places. In Lost Creek, Pennsylvania, union stalwarts offered three elderly union officers from $100 to $500, on several occasions, to "stimulate for Boyle, Titler and Owens." John Karlavage, the UMW field representative who contacted the men, said he did the same in 30 other locals "from Shenandoah clear down to Shamekin," a distance of about 25 miles. These weren't payoffs; rather, they were "reimbursements for expenses and missed work time," he said, adding nonchalantly, "Quite a few accepted."

Another well-placed UMW field worker passed out "good-will money" of $300 to $400 to miners. He acknowledged his dispersals totaled about $3,000. (Karlavage put his at $2,800.) The expenditures went for such diverse activities as picking up the tab at nightclubs ($240 on one occasion) to paying miners $50 to drive union members to the polls on election day. The source of these funds is somewhat mysterious. Union testimony indicates its origin as the "Boyle-Titler-Owens" campaign fund, supposedly made up of donations collected from union loyalists. It does not disclose the amount and composite use of these funds.

On the Stump

At 59, Jock Yablonski looked the part of the coal-digger politician. His bushy eyebrows and balloonlike nose dominated his face. His skin was creviced with the lines of middle age, but his shoulders were muscled like those of a man 20 years younger. When he sat still, he was shrouded by smoke from the pencil-thin cigars and cigarettes that he puffed constantly. When he moved, it was with a quick, hard handshake and a bellow: "My name is Jock Yablonski. I'm gonna straighten this union out. I hope you can see your way clear to vote for me."

His campaign was financed on a shoestring. His staff was an unlikely assortment of dissident coal miners, college students, professional crusaders and his family, including his two sons, Joseph, Jr., and Kenneth, Charlotte, his social-worker daughter, and his wife, Margaret. While Boyle traveled first class with a large staff and a seemingly endless supply of money, Yablonski drove from mine to mine in his Chevy, often accompanied only by his nephew, Eddie Yablonski, a high-school social-studies teacher and ex-Marine. His days often stretched 18 hours. Always, they'd be topped off with a double scotch on the rocks "to help me sleep."

Sometimes he'd be joined by his vice-presidential running mate, Elmer Brown. Other times, Dr. Halwey Wells of Morgantown, West Virginia, flew him to rallies in his private plane. Before one such trip, Wells found his gas tank stuffed with leaves and pine cones, apparently the work of a would-be assassin.

In the old Lewis tradition, Yablonski spoke without notes, often reciting lengthy statistics from memory. Frequently he lapsed into outbursts of profanity. As he talked, he'd loosen his tie. Off would come his suit coat, and his left hand would tug at his trousers, hitching them up to keep them from sagging below his paunch. Occasionally, late in the day, he would concede he was prepared to lose because "the incumbent union leadership plans to steal the election." Then he'd pause, and add:

> We've made them get out of their swivel chairs and made them come into the areas where the dust is and meet the men who dig the coal and pay their salaries, and by God you know that they would never have gotten out of their swivel chairs and come down into the boondocks if it hadn't been for us being a candidate.

After an initial period of brooding, Boyle forces did indeed give up their swivel chairs. ("Tony was just sitting around; finally our safety director went in and told him, 'Get off your ass, get out there with the rank and file,'" one UMW spokesman explained.) Ambitious tours through the coalfields with frequent speaking engagements were announced—many labeled "mine safety" or "black lung" rallies and paid for with union funds. By Labor Day, Boyle had hired an expensive political publicist who wrote a platform that Boyle delivered at Elkhorn City, Kentucky. Designed to mute Yablonski attacks, the platform adopted many of the reforms proposed by the challenger. Had it not been given by Boyle himself, it could have been interpreted as a stinging indictment of a union that hadn't kept pace with the times.

Two issues Boyle didn't touch—corruption and union autonomy. These were Yablonski's issues. As Yablonski promised reform, he predicted Boyle would end up in jail. "He's going to end up a cellmate of Jimmy Hoffa," he declared at a rally in Madisonville, Kentucky.

Autonomy was a less dramatic but equally important issue. How could a miner depend on his union to stick up for him when his district officers are appointed by someone in Washington instead of elected by the men who dig coal? How could a miner make such men do anything about mines that aren't safe to work? "How democratic is an organization," Yablonski asked, "when a man who's served it for 35 years announces he's going to become a candidate for office, and they hire an expert karate thug to hit him from behind in order to try to paralyze him! That's what happened to me in Springfield, Illinois."

The appeal was emotional; the words, common sense. Where they worked, they worked well. In Pennsylvania, Ohio, northern and central West Virginia and Illinois (where he refused to campaign after the karate incident), working miners flocked to Yablonski's rallies. These men were the sons and grandsons of immigrants who had come to the American coalfields seeking the good life. Their union had been the nation's most militant, truly at the vanguard of American labor. It wasn't afraid to spit in the eye of the big coal bosses or raid their purses for wages and fringe benefits thought out of the question by other unions. These men were justifiably proud of the union and had tried to preserve some vestiges of democracy in it. As the 1960's drew to a close, their coalfields were the only ones in the nation with some degree of local control.

In central Appalachia, it was a different story. The UMW —like everything else—had been a latecomer here. Many mines weren't organized until the 1930's and 1940's. Democratic traditions didn't develop as they had in the older mining areas. Indeed, democratic models were hard to come by. Corruption and vote fraud were still accepted as part of life. The rugged terrain and the rule of the coal companies hemmed the miners in. New ideas and social movements were slow in developing.

The miners themselves differed. While newly immigrated Welsh, Poles, Italians, Hungarians and Slovaks made up the payrolls of mines in other parts of the country, the labor force in central Appalachia came from the surrounding hills. Their ties were to their kin and their hollow, not to the union. For them, Lewis was the union, and Tony Boyle, who skillfully played on the Lewis legend, was Lewis's man. "I ain't going to vote for no hunkie," a retired miner in Floyd County, Kentucky, told me that fall. "Lewis picked Tony Boyle. He knowed what he was doing, that's good enough for me."

In central Appalachia apathy and fear greeted Yablonski.

At Pikeville, Kentucky, he could attract only 50 people to a rally in the county courthouse. Later, Yablonski carefully skirted the large eastern Kentucky coalfields for fear of his life after an ad in the nearby Williamson, West Virginia, *Daily* warned: "Stay out of District 30 Joseph Yablonski and Elmer Brown." By election day, one miner would comment, "There's been more talk on this in the television than in the mines."

Boyle's strategy? Oil the machine and divide the op-positon. Discredit the insurgent. Question his personal motives and personal life. Play on the greatness of the past, the legacy of the sacred Lewis legend. Warn of threats to the future. Tony Boyle put it all in one speech at Madisonville, Kentucky, a week before the election:

> Joseph Yablonski lies through his teeth. He talks with two tongues. . . . Because he is guilty of lies, defamation of John L. Lewis, conflict of interest and antiunion acts, Joseph Yablonski is unfit to be president of the United Mine Workers union. He will be rejected by the membership as a power-hungry opportunist and hypocrite . . . he stoops low indeed in his smear campaign. While his smear appears to be directed toward me and the other top officers of the UMW, the real target is John L. Lewis.

This was old politics, machine politics waged with a vengeance. Its practitioners were the union stalwarts who depended on the Boyle regime for jobs, many of them the same men who had been union mainstays during bloody organizing drives.

The Yablonski effort was an exercise in "new politics." It was based on the supposition that a wave of indignation—actually more of a mild breeze—was sweeping Appalachia. The oppressed of the nation's poorest region were demanding social justice, a chance at a decent life and a voice in their own destiny, the theory went. Coal miners, workers in the nation's most dangerous occupation, were a vital part of this wave. They wanted safer mines, more security and control over their own union.

Their strategists were Washington liberals and coalfield professionals—such men as civil libertarian Joseph Rauh, Jr., comsumer crusader Ralph Nader, and Congressman Ken Hechler, an outspoken former college professor. They were political idealists, men who had been on the right side of many good causes. Their theory was that miners, when presented with an attractive candidate and documentation of widespread corruption, would throw the old-line union leadership out. Their workers were volunteers; their communication system, a sympathetic press.

The Labor Department, which was supposed to oversee the election, understood neither the old nor the new politics. When it acted, it acted feebly. When it didn't act, which was almost all the time, it showed all the indecision of a bureaucracy at its worst.

In the meantime, college students, reformers and journalists flocked to the Yablonski camp. They wrote articles, moaned over cocktails and visited coal miners. And, they didn't seem to understand when the miners didn't respond with the same enthusiasm.

Jock Yablonski, the old union politician, the eloquent wheeler-dealer, became his workers' folk hero, their tie to the coalfields. Yablonski adopted their thoughts and ways. As the months progressed, the campaign increasingly took on the look of a holy crusade. His enemies said he had been brainwashed by outsiders. His friends said he had been moved by the plight of the miners and their widows.

"Jock grew. If he wasn't convinced with what he was doing at the start, he became so as the months passed," said one observer. "I don't really think he knew how bad it was, how deep the anger." Even his vice-presidential running mate, who had long harbored personal misgivings, was won over in the end. "He saw the plight of the coal miners and he became sincere," Brown said.

With just over a week remaining before the election, Yablonski fired two final salvos. The first was a letter to the Labor Department, which a few days before had released a report charging Boyle with mishandling union funds. In the letter, attorney Joseph Rauh made a final plea for government intervention in the election, documenting massive irregularities, including a union admission that it had printed more than 50,000 extra ballots and a statement by a federal judge that the ballots were being handled "kind of willy-nilly." "The failure of the Department of Labor to take strong measures to insure a fair election may well bring in its train ugly violence in the mines," the letter warned.

The second blast was a lawsuit accusing Boyle and other top union officials of misspending "many millions of dollars." Among specific allegations: union officials used up to $9 million of UMW funds for questionable investments and loans; Boyle had diverted hundreds of thousands of dollars for his own self-aggrandizement; Boyle had used loans to UMW districts to manipulate the organization and stack union conventions with his sympathizers; Boyle had spent untold thousands more union dollars during the campaign for vote buying and placing his supporters on the UMW payroll. Boyle called the suit, which at this writing is still pending, "cheap harassment."

The Election

On December 9, miners in southern West Virginia voted in a light drizzle. In Kentucky, a cold wind blew eastward across the bluegrass toward the Cumberland Plateau. Two inches of snow blanketed the roofs of polling places in Nova Scotia.

Jock Yablonski rose early and voted at 9:30 A.M. at the Polish Hall at California, Pennsylvania, fully confident the election was his. Tony Boyle spent the day in his home in northwest Washington, D.C. He scribbled his choice on an absentee ballot from his home local in Billings, Montana.

Throughout the coalfields, cars driven by Boyle supporters, many of them paid up to $50 for their efforts, carried voters to polling places in schoolhouses and private homes. Yablonski had observers at about two-thirds of the polling places. In Fairmont, West Virginia, one such observer recalls, "They carried men in who couldn't walk. The Boyle men brought in one retired miner who couldn't see, walk or read and told him 'sign it here.'" In local 9938 in Nova Scotia, Canada, an investigation found, miners weren't even given a chance to vote, although the UMW reported they had given Boyle a 150-to-5-vote margin.

The polls officially closed at 6 P.M. in the East. At 2 A.M., Boyle issued a victory statement from the offices of the UMW *Journal*. The miners had answered, he said, "to those outside forces seeking to substitute their judgment and values for those of the men who have risked life and limb to dig the nation's coal."

"They can go to hell," retorted Yablonski, declaring the election the "most dishonest in the history of the American labor movement." "I'm conceding to nobody. I'm conceding nothing."

Official returns later showed Boyle had won by 34,504 votes, almost a 2-to-1 margin. He carried 22 of the union's 25 districts, including Yablonski's home territory in southwestern Pennsylvania. The challenger had done well among working miners and where he had poll watchers. But he had lost an estimated 93 percent of the pensioner vote. In 303 predominately pensioner locals, he failed to collect a single vote. In 98 percent of these, he had no poll watchers.

Yablonski contested the figures before they were even released. In an official challenge, he wrote, "Tony Boyle stole the election . . . his campaign can best be described as a great treasury raid in which he converted the dues of honest mine workers and elderly pensioners to his personal campaign and used the personnel of the UMW as though they were his private servants."

Jock Yablonski had one final rally five days after the election. It was held on an icy Sunday in the Sophia, West Virginia, High School auditorium. Driving was hazardous and the crowd small—about 300, mostly those who had worked closest to the campaign. "I've accomplished more in the last seven months," he told the faithful, "than I did in the past 35 years in the union."

A couple of days later, he called his vice-presidential running mate, Elmer Brown. "He said something big was coming up," Brown remembers. "He didn't say what. Only that he wanted me to stay in the clear so I could take over the union if something happened to him."

That was the last Brown heard from Yablonski. On December 31, sometime after midnight, three men crept to the second floor of Yablonski's fieldstone house at the end of a lonely road near Clarksville, Pennsylvania. One of them fired a .38 caliber revolver slug into Charlotte Yablonski's head. Yablonski reached for a double-barreled shotgun he kept near the bed. A second gunman cut him down. When his body was found six days later, there were four .38 caliber slugs in it. A fifth was found in the floor of the master bedroom. His wife, Margaret, had been shot twice.

Part 2

Of Decay and Callousness

These are my people, these poor, hurt people, with hunger in their eyes. These people, who stand tall and proud, and who haven't forgotten how to laugh. These people who accept change slowly, who have nothing to show for all the years of hard work. Who raise their families in shacks, who have little to eat, and are cold because the wind blows through the holes in their clothes. These warm-hearted, loving people, who suffer and fight in silence, these proud and beautiful people who make life worth living just because they are: MY PEOPLE.

Sharon Dixon, senior
Letcher High School
Letcher County, Kentucky 1970

9

The Old Hillbilly

Sherman Hensley lives at the foot of a mountain in the far western edge of Virginia, about 15 miles from the Cumberland Gap. His daughter-in-law, Stella, calls the place "an old rockhouse." Actually it's a four-room frame cabin, not unlike its nearest neighbor half a mile away. Sherman didn't want to move there in the first place. He didn't want to come off the mountain. When he did, he didn't come far. Just about where a rock would naturally come to rest if you threw it off the mountaintop.

"I thought it was right healthy up on that mountain," he'll say thoughtfully if you ask about it. "Kind of a peaceable place up there."

Then he'll pause and look out the window at the clear spring that bubbles from the side of the hill by his house and add, "Never did like being in public much anyway."

Sherman is small and thin. He has gray hair and the tightly drawn, craggy skin that comes from living to be 91 years old. A worn hickory cane leans against the wall in the kitchen. But he looks as if he could still tramp up Cumberland Mountain if he had half a mind to.

I first met him on one of those sunny, warm January days that sometimes come to the Cumberland Mountains in midwinter, melting the snow from the hillsides and slicking the roads with mud. I had been looking, somewhat foolishly, for two weeks for an untainted "old hillbilly," someone who would represent the best traits of the proud, fiercely independent, Anglo-Saxon mountaineer. This proved no easy task. It's one of those quirks of today that it is easier to find lovebeads and bellbottom trousers in most mountain counties than a mountaineer unblemished by "progress." "The Welfare done got them all," the shopkeepers in the county seats told me. Or, "Five years ago I could have found you a dozen or more—fine folks who wouldn't take a handout for nothing—but that generation, they all died out."

So the trail went from county to county, talking, loafing, eating with old people. Admiring the quiet, polite serenity the hills had given them. Listening to the tales they were eager to tell. Reaffirming that people don't fit into convenient stereotyped niches, whether they be "feudin' moonshiners from Appalachia" or Jewish mothers from the Bronx.

One morning I found myself at Sherman Hensley's place, not with the idea that he was a typical "old hillbilly," but simply wanting to meet a man who moved onto a mountain almost 70 years ago and never really moved off.

Sherman's life on the mountain started quite unspectacularly when he bought 38.2 acres atop Brush and Cumberland mountains from his father-in-law, Burton Hensley. Sherman had been born in Harlan County, Kentucky, and spent enough time in one-room schools there to learn to read and write. For a few years he had been a rural mail carrier, taking the mail from farm to farm on horseback. But mostly he was a farmer.

One day in 1904 he loaded his young bride, Burton Hensley's daughter, Nicey Ann, in a mule-drawn wagon with a few possessions and they started the treacherous climb up the Kentucky side of Cumberland Mountain toward what would become known as Hensley Flats, or Hensley Settlement.

"I'd been up there before," Sherman recalled. "I sawed it was a good hog range. Thought I'd try it awhile and I stayed 48 years. Went mostly to make some money raising hogs in the chestnuts. Hogs get fatter on chestnuts than corn, yah know."

Sherman's voice was clear and slow. He weighed each word with the care of a diplomat.

"Raised a right smart amount of hogs up there," he continued. "Never had no fences or pens. Just let 'em run. Mighty good place to raise hogs. Mighty good place to lose 'em, too."

Sherman and Nicey Ann built their farm near the center of a 508-acre plateau. The cabin, where Nicey Ann reared 19 children, was fashioned from rough-hewn logs. Its walls, eight inches thick, were made of stripped logs laid end-to-end atop one another and then caulked with mud. A second layer of flat boards in varying lengths was stuck on the outside walls with mud to give added protection from the weather. A stone fireplace was at one end of the cabin. Split-log floorboards covered the floor.

Eventually more families, mostly Hensleys and their in-laws the Gibbons, moved to Hensley Flats, and the population grew to 160 by the 1930's. But when Sherman and

Nicey Ann arrived, the entire plateau was largely untouched by man. Virgin growth of chestnut, hickory, beech and poplar covered the hillsides. Possums, squirrels, coons, deer, polecats and turkeys ran wild.

Life was hard in the settlement. For the men, there were barns, smokehouses, cabins and outdoor privies to build, land to clear, hogs to slaughter, crops to harvest, tools and furniture to make, game to hunt. For the women, there were endless meals to cook, vegetables to can, clothes to sew, gardens to hoe, children to raise. There were no televisions or radios or telephones—or even electricity for that matter. Everyone rose at 5:00 or 6:00 A.M., worked all day and retired at 8:00 or 9:00 P.M., "Unless we had company."

"I don't know if I'd do it again," Sherman said. "I'm not educated. I had to work hard, real hard every day for my livin'. I still believe I made a mistake goin' up there. Always wonder if we couldn't done better somewhere else."

The settlement was almost totally self-sufficient through the mid-1940's. It had its own cane mill, two other water-driven mills and a blacksmith shop that produced farm implements and building tools. Willie Gibbons, the blacksmith, made household furniture for much of the community. A 40-inch coal seam provided a ready supply of fuel.

Women handsewed their cotton dresses. Men wore store-bought "Kentucky Jeans," a tough, gray wool trouser, and handmade gray-and-white "hickory shirts" so durable "You could wear it every day of the year and it'd never wear out." Both sexes wore plain, rough-sewn "Brog Shoes," which could fit either the right or left foot.

Aside from coffee, tea and baking soda, few foodstuffs had to be bought. Each farm raised its own corn, beans, tomatoes, peas, cucumbers, hanovers (a type of rhutabaga) and potatoes. Huckleberries grew wild. Hogs, sheep and some cattle roamed the hillsides freely, each identifiable only by the notch or brand that its owner had cut in its left ear.

Sherman owned up to 100 hogs at times, making him well-off by settlement standards. Sometimes he wouldn't see some of them for months, and when he wanted to slaughter one, he'd have to hunt it down. It was on one of these trips that Sherman Hensley killed his Indian. He won't discuss it himself. He's too moral and God-fearing for that. But, according to his son Wallace, it happened one day when Sherman and one of the Gibbons were rounding up hogs. Unbeknownst to them, an Indian awaiting trial for murder had taken up residence on a nearby mountain. The Hensleys didn't know the Indian and the Indian didn't know them, so when they ran into each other in a grove of trees both were surprised. The runaway Indian immediately mistook Sherman and his companion for law enforcement agents out to arrest him.

Sherman tried to persuade him otherwise, but the Indian wouldn't listen. He pointed his rifle and threatened to kill both of them. Sherman grabbed for the barrel and went tumbling down the mountainside with the struggling Indian still at the other end of the gun. Just when Sherman wrestled the gun away, the Indian lunged at him. Sherman fired. The Indian fell dead. The Bell County, Kentucky, sheriff investigated and found the shooting to be self defense. Sherman helped bury the Indian, but he never mentioned the incident to his family.

"It's one of those things he didn't want none of us to know about," Wallace said. "I would never have known if someone else hadn't told me. I tell you my dad is a clean liver. He never belonged to no church. But he's a moral man, a real moral man. He wanted us to be the same way."

The Hensley Flats were too isolated to have many such problems. It is a 90-minute hike up a steep grade to reach the old settlement from the Virginia side of the mountain. The trail up the Kentucky side is less treacherous, but longer. Few attempted to trek up either, and it was 1956 before the first motor vehicle, a four-wheel-drive jeep, made it to the plateau.

Sherman and the rest of the Hensleys made little effort to cultivate contacts with the outside world. They left the mountain for the small cities of Middlesboro and Pineville, Kentucky, only when they had to vote (Sherman is a lifelong Republican), to shop, to pick up mail or to transact necessary business. Women sometimes left as seldom as three or four times a year. Men went frequently, some every week. One group of younger men and older boys, for instance, rode their horses and mules down to the country store at Caylor, Virginia, near where Sherman now lives, every Saturday afternoon. As Wallace remembers it, the men would keep their mounts "slicked down like a bluegrass racehorse" for the outings, and the Hensleys would always pay cash. "That storekeeper was mighty glad to see us," he says.

When trouble did arise, the clan dealt with it in its own way. Usually, Sherman, the patriarch of the Hensley family, would meet with Willie Gibbons, the patriarch of the Gibbons family, and a few other heads of families, and decide what action to take. It was seldom necessary to take such steps.

"Because some live in the mountains, people think they're outlaws, but that's not true," Sherman said. "We had less trouble with violence on that mountain than anywhere. And if real trouble came up we had law and order. We had an officer to get. You could call him anytime."

The "officer," apparently a deputy county sheriff, was never called, however. The reason was obvious. Sherman and nearly every other man in the settlement operated stills.

They depended on moonshine whiskey as their chief source of outside income. It sold for $10 a gallon, and the money went for things like paying grocery bills and buying new mules to plow corn. Jeopardizing this industry by inviting deputy sheriffs around would have been pure folly.

Most often "the law" left Hensley Flat moonshiners alone —if for no other reason than they were simply too far away to bother with. But several enforcement officers did visit the plateau. Court records indicate that on several occasions different residents were fined for making illegal whiskey. And legend has it that once a Bell County sheriff rode all the way up the mountain only to be so overwhelmed by the Hensley hospitality and good whiskey that he forgot to make a single arrest.

The Hensleys today have ambivalent feelings about their moonshining days. Sherman, for instance, still boasts about the fine quality of the settlement's clear white corn whiskey. "It was purer than what you get nowadays," he says. "Nowadays they go putting chemicals in it. It's not real liquor. They gotten to artisfishicating it."

When the question of moonshining comes up, they make sure you understand that they did it simply because it was the only way to earn cash. Then they'll pause, searching for reassurance, and ask: "I've been studying right smart on this, reading the Bible and such. Do you think the Lord understands?"

The Hensley Settlement never had an organized church. Religion in the primitive, fundamentalist state that permeates the entire Appalachian region was most often passed from mother to daughter by word of mouth and the family Bible. Itinerant preachers would drop by several times a year to rekindle the fires of salvation and damnation. But the only regularly scheduled services were held on "Dedication

Day," a Sunday set aside each spring for religious ceremonies. As many as four preachers would preside over these special services and put the church's blessings on all baptisms, marriages and funerals that had taken place during the year.

Recreation was limited. Men had horseback riding, hunting and Sunday softball games. Occasionally some of the younger ones would take a jug of moonshine whiskey over the hill and "tie one on" on Saturday nights. Women had quilting bees, bean shellings and "visitin'." They washed clothes on crude scrubboards. When a traveling salesman tried to sell several of them handwringer washing machines, they laughed at him. "We didn't think it could get clothes clean," one explained. "We just didn't know no better."

Education happened in a one-room log schoolhouse that first opened in 1912. Eight grades were offered at the school, but the children seldom went past the fourth year. Teachers were hired by the Bell County school system. They boarded in the settlement. Sherman was the school's trustee, and his son, Wallace, married one of the pretty young schoolmarms who came up the mountain to teach.

What Wallace's wife remembers most about the settlement is the hard work and how people helped one another. "Them was good old days," she said in her warm, soft school teacher voice. "We didn't have any money, but we never went hungry. We were poor people, but we was industrious. We never did want any welfare. We had too much pride in us. We wasn't like the grasshopper. We knew if you didn't put any away, you wouldn't have it."

The settlement began a slow death with the start of World War II. Its men had always spent a few days each year working outside the farm community, mining coal, timbering and repairing county roads. But the wages were small and the work backbreaking. The war changed that. Some of the younger men joined the army. Others found new, higher paying jobs in nearby coal mines and in not-so-near defense plants. The work and pay were far better than anything they could remember on the mountain, and when the war ended, they didn't return to the old homesteads. "The easy life sinks in on you," one explained.

Sherman soon found himself among a dwindling group of diehards on the plateau. One by one his old friends died off. Their sons and daughters moved away, leaving the settlement ever more quiet, ever more lonely. By 1946 attendance had fallen so much that the school was abandoned, thus causing several more families to leave.

Sherman probably would have stayed forever if the Kentucky Park Commission hadn't bought all the land on the flats in the late 1940's. As it was, he was the only one living on it when the sale was made, and he stayed two years alone on the mountain. The Park Commission had promised him he could remain on the land for the rest of his life, but Sherman has never really trusted government, so one day he "took a notion to move off." His children had hoped that he would move in with one of them or find a small place in nearby Middlesboro, Kentucky, close to modern conveniences. But instead Sherman bought a cabin at the end of a desolate clay path at the foot of the mountain where he had spent most of his life. He insisted, just as he had ever since Nicey Ann died in 1936, that he live alone. "Jest drather have a place of my own," he explained. "Jest don't like to be crowded."

It was after midday, and Sherman was tiring as we sat on his couch across the room from a calendar from Davidson Funeral Home in Rose Hill, Virginia, and a black-and-white sign that said, "Jesus Never Fails." But Sherman hadn't lost his zeal for conversation. His voice still slow, still firm, he talked about the Vietnam War (he was against it—"It's killing a lot of our boys."), hippies (he'd like to meet one), welfare and his philosophy of life.

"First a man oughta live honest," he said. "Let what he gets come by it honestly. I don't believe in defraudin' anyone. If it's worth havin', it's worth earnin' right. People should teach their children that, to be honest, and not to violate the laws of the land."

Sherman listens to the news on television. He doesn't watch it because his eyes hurt him. He worries about Vietnam and student protesters and murders and what way the country is going. But mostly he worries about the people around him.

"People have changed to a different way of life," he said. "Used to have more good people than we do now. Wasn't as much lawin', killin' and confusion. We got more mean people than we used to.

"Too many folks turn to this welfare, lookin' to someone else to take up for them. In a way it's good for those that don't have nothin', but on the other hand lots draw it that's got enough to live on anyway."

"I never took a penny," he added. "And I don't want it. Never asked for it. Don't think that's honest.

"In my judgment we should go back to our ways," Sherman said.

10

Welfare

It was check day, the first of the month. The dust-caked Chevy and Ford sedans and the International Harvester pickups bounced down Main Street from the sandstone courthouse on the hill to the grimy business district a block and a half below. The street had been almost deserted the day before, but now traffic was bumper to bumper and parking spots were almost impossible to find.

At the First State Bank on the corner of Bridge Street and Town Square, tellers faced the busiest day of the month. There would be Aid to Families with Dependent Children (AFDC) checks for mothers with dependent children, Social Security checks for the elderly, disability checks for those permanently injured, "John L. Lewis" checks for a few retired union miners and veterans checks for old soldiers. There would be at least one for every four people in Clay

County, Kentucky. They had to be cashed so their bearers could buy their monthly quota of food stamps or pay their next month's rent.

The bank and almost every other business were more than happy to cash them. The businessmen of Manchester, Kentucky, are practical men. They realize that they operate in a one-industry economy. And that industry, whether they like it or not, is welfare. The checks form the backbone of their economy. They go for food at Dobson's Grocery, drugs at the Porter-Ely Walgreen agency, cigarettes, car payments, clothes and most anything else that it takes to keep a family alive in one of the most remote areas of eastern Kentucky.

"Welfare is all we've got. There just isn't any industry here," Pete Chestnut, the young manager of the Southern Dollar Store on Main Street, was saying. "A person can't get a job if he wants one, and these people want to work. Every week five or six come by this place looking for a job. Yesterday this girl was here. Well-groomed, nice girl with three years of college. Her husband left her with a kid and she needed work. Said she'd work for anything—75 cents an hour, anything, just so she would get off welfare. I'm full up with help and so is everyone else in town. So where does a girl like that turn but to welfare?"

Check day is the day welfare comes to town. The pensioners, the blind, the crippled and the needy from every corner of the county descend on the county seat *en masse*. It's like payday in a Pennsylvania milltown, Saturday night on an Iowa courthouse square and a sale at Macy's all rolled into one.

"If you haven't been in Manchester at the first of the month you've never seen a real traffic jam," Chestnut said. "Cars wait half an hour without moving an inch. It's worse than Cincinnati any day, I swear. They've got traffic lights there. We haven't got a one here."

It was 9:30 A.M., and the rush had just begun.

"You come back by at eleven o'clock and you wouldn't be able to walk through this place. The checkout line will be clear back to that wall," he said.

Chestnut, whose wife works for the state department of public assistance, understands mountain economics. His father, who runs a secondhand furniture store, taught him decades ago that the welfare dollar is as good—and much more plentiful—than any other dollar. There is a certain amount of cunning involved, however.

"Here you either make it the first 15 days of the month or not at all," he explained. "It's dead around here the last of the month. That welfare money doesn't last long. If you're going to get it, you have to get it right fast."

Chestnut had put on extra help for the day. His shelves were stacked two and three feet high with merchandise with 98-cent, $1.58 and $2.98 price tags. Several clerks were uncrating a fresh shipment of clothes—thin cotton dresses, denims and cheap shoes mostly—in the back room. He was determined to get his fair slice of the welfare dollar.

So were the Saylor Brothers at their modern supermarket a block away. "We Gladly Accept Food Stamps," read a sign on their front door.

"Sure the food stamps help us; not as much as some stores because we're in the middle of town and we get lot of trade from the townspeople," said Doug Saylor. "But without them we'd be hurting. So would a lot of places. Imagine some would go out of business without them."

A block away 6 lines of people, each line 25 to 30 people deep, spilled out of the old storefront that serves as the county food-stamp office onto Town Square Street. Most were shabbily dressed. Their faces were solemn, their lips tight. There were craggy-faced men, old women with hunched backs, young women with babies in their arms, good people, bad people, devout people, drunks and hard workers. People with names like Combs, Justice, Chandler, Messer, Owens, Childres. Each clasped in one hand an envelope containing a few dollar bills and a green computer card entitling him to his monthly ration of food stamps.

Paul Hudson, a coal miner from Paces Creek who hadn't worked in nine months, said he didn't know how he could survive without the $84 worth of food stamps he purchased for $40 each month.

"There'd be a lot of children go hungry if it weren't fer them. I know there would," said a lanky farmer with seven children from Big Bullskin Creek in line behind Hudson.

A woman in a dirty red-cloth coat from Ice House Creek agreed. "I've got five young 'uns," she said. "I couldn't feed them without stamps. We don't even have no milk. That's the reason I came today. We need food. My husband's crippled. He can't get no work nowhere."

Harto Womblies, from Goose Rock, felt pretty much the same way, but he wasn't sure about other welfare programs. "I worked all my life until I got sick and the doctor told me my back was tored all to hell. I don't have no income now. Can't get to drawin' on anything even though I can't work. Someone's gettin' it somewhere. It's got to be crooked. Otherwise I'd be drawin' some."

Among the townsfolk of every mountain community, there are many explanations of why so many people are "drawin' rather than workin'." Most revolve around middle-class mis-conceptions: that recipients are freeloading on public dole; that they are "too sorry," or lazy, to work; that they are illiterate degenerates lacking education and motivation; or that welfare programs are set up so it is more profitable to loaf than work.

No one can deny that the welfare system in Appalachia and the rest of the nation is a dismal failure, or that it doesn't produce a certain amount of con-artistry and a great deal of waste. But most people miss the central truth of why so many people in Clay County and every other Appalachian county depend on welfare: simply that they made the mistake of being born to the wrong parents, in the wrong section of the country.

Clay County has a greater appreciation of this than most places. Only 5 of the 120 counties in Kentucky, a state that consistently ranks among the nation's poorest, had lower per capita incomes in 1970. Aside from a few scattered truck mines, Clay County has no industry. There simply isn't any place for a man to work and there hasn't been for two decades. Welfare is the only place to turn for a livelihood. And today much of the county is in its third welfare generation.

In dollar terms, the cost is appalling. Even the well-oiled computers in the Kentucky Department of Economic Security, which administers most welfare programs, have a hard time keeping up with the constant outflow of tax dollars.

In one month, they suggested 4,020 recipients were paid $153,359. During this month, 806 old people were handed aid-to-the-aged checks totaling $45,846; 303 of the permanently disabled collected more than $22,000; 147 of the needy blind received $11,759; and 679 families with almost 2,000 children collected AFDC checks totaling more than $73,000.

These figures just scratch the surface of the dole. They fail to consider, for example, that two-thirds of the county's children receive their school lunches at no cost or at reduced prices because they can't afford to pay for them; or that two out of every five families receive food stamps worth a total of $234,680 each month; or that government medical programs cost an average of $67,000 each 30 days; or that the local antipoverty agency dispensed emergency food and medical vouchers worth $3,700 to families each month before it was shut down for political interference.

Far more tragic is the human cost. Welfare has become a way of life for thousands of mountaineers. It has sapped their ambition and destroyed their pride. In the process, it has created its own culture, a culture that old hillbillies like Stewart Hensley would scarcely recognize. It is a culture of dependency. In it, welfare isn't just a fact, it is a special way of life, with its own cynical view of reality. This view and the attitudes it breeds affect everything a welfare recipient does, from the way he regards sex to what he buys to eat at the first of each month.

Welfare has created a dead-end culture. Everything works against a child born into it. The meager check his mother receives isn't enough to house or feed him properly, so he suffers from malnutrition. Because he suffers from malnutrition, he gets sick, but proper medical care is not available. So he is often sick and often misses school. School has little meaning for him, anyway. His mother doesn't have money to buy the books and toys that other children have. Soon he loses all interest. Even if his mother is able to give him an adequate diet, keep him in school and administer to his medical needs, by the time he reaches his early teens, he finds he doesn't have enough money to buy the kind of clothes other children wear. He's embarrassed by his poverty and drops out. There is little in the welfare culture to indicate to him that education is worthwhile, anyway. Even if he does complete school, in a place like Clay County there are no jobs available for him. His schools have not prepared him to live anywhere else. In the unlikely event that he finds a job, an untimely accident or illness may suddenly thrust him back into the vicious cycle, around and around, toward even more suffering and poverty.

Dorothy Taylor

There are many such victims of the welfare culture in Clay County. Some have dropped so far downward it is unlikely they will ever bounce back. Many of them have given up. A few still have hope. Dorothy Taylor is one of them.

At 26, she is still pretty. Her body is slender, her hair cropped boyishly short. She has a long classic mountain nose, with blue eyes set back in her head. Her manner is frank and self-assured.

"By my part, I'm getting along pretty good by what other people got," she said.

She stood shivering in a corner of the two-room clapboard box on Powderhorn Mountain that she and her four children call home. The cold January wind seeped through the walls around her. The fire in the kitchen had died out hours before, just after the two oldest Taylor children—Kenneth, 7, and Janice, 6—had left for the treacherous 1½-mile journey down the mountain to meet the bus from Goose Rock School.

It was 3:00 P.M. In another hour Mrs. Taylor would start the fire so the children could be warm when they returned from school. Or maybe she would wait. Coal cost $11.50 a ton. It shouldn't be wasted. In the meantime, the other two Taylor children—Edward, 4, the one with the dirty face and soiled red pullover, and Linda, 5, born with no legs and only one arm—were spending the afternoon at her mother-in-law's place about halfway down the slope toward Mill Creek.

Dorothy was only a teenager when she married George

Taylor, a man twice her age. She was a school dropout at 13, one of eight children in a family that had never known anything but poverty. Her parents had separated, and her father was killed in a squabble over family land. George Taylor was well off by comparison. He owned a piece of property on Powderhorn Mountain that he farmed when he wasn't working at odd jobs. He died unexpectedly at 47. "We had him in three hospitals; doctors could never figure out what it was," she said.

Dorothy was 24, the mother of four, when George died. She reluctantly decided to stay on the mountain because her mother-in-law and her husband's land were there. "As for my part goes, I wouldn't give two cents to live here otherwise," she said.

Her life now revolves around her children. She wakes them at 5:00 A.M. and prepares a hot breakfast of oatmeal and corn biscuits. By 7, they are on their way to school. She spends the rest of the day with the two younger children, sometimes at her mother-in-law's house, sometimes at her own. About once a week she will walk to the post office at Bright Shade for mail or to shop at Pearl Hubbard's grocery. Both are an hour's hike away. Twice a month she hires a neighbor for $3 to drive her to Manchester, once to pick up food stamps. There is little time or money for recreation. Her home has no television or radio.

"I can't have a good time. I just stay in the house day in and day out," Mrs. Taylor said. "Sometimes I think it's a pretty bad life. Then again it's pretty good taking care of four young'uns.

"If I had a different life I wouldn't want to stay here," she continued. "I want my family to be happy when they grow up. I want them to have a better education than me." (If they do, their education will indicate great powers of endurance.

It takes her two small children more than three hours each day to travel to and from school, including two hours on foot over some of the roughest terrain in Appalachia.)

"They like school," Mrs. Taylor said reassuringly when I asked her about the travel time. "I think they might make it."

She looked frightfully alone, terribly alien to the world most of us know. All the worldly possessions that a $165-a-month AFDC check can buy were in the room around her. There wasn't much: two old double beds with faded quilts; a dilapidated gray sofa with the stuffing from one cushion spilling out; a stove on which she makes a $13.70 payment each month; three wire coat hangers holding her children's extra clothes; two red tinsel Christmas wreaths; a blue boy's parka stuffed between the yellow linoleum floor and the bottom of the front door; two bare light bulbs; and a worn lady's boot, half hidden under one bed.

Most of the furnishings have been donated by relatives. Dorothy Taylor can't afford to buy any herself. She can afford to buy almost nothing. Her check is too small.

"Oh, I can feed my family, but I have to go into debt each month to do it," she said.

The size of welfare allotments is always a subject of controversy in mountain counties. Those who don't get monthly checks maintain they're too high, that a good man can do better living off dole than working. Those who do get checks say they're too low. I side with the latter. The typical AFDC family with three children receives $187 a month in Kentucky. This is calculated on a 73.1-percent-of-need basis, which means welfare grants by definition pay less than three-fourths of what it is supposed to take to live on. By contrast the same family would receive $336 if it lived in New York state, $263 in Michigan.

President Nixon's welfare-reform package would offer little immediate help for most Kentucky welfare recipients. Dorothy Taylor's family, for instance, would receive $200, just $35 more than she receives without it.

Toleman Jackson

By Toleman Jackson's own account, "any family that ain't gittin' $300 a month ain't livin'." By this same account, he said, "Reckon we ain't been livin' for 'bout seven years."

Jackson was in his favorite rocking chair, fingering the gray stubble on his chin. The fireplace in front of his knees threw off a warm red glow. He stabbed a poker into the fire.

"We don't draw but $150 a month," he said. "A man can't live on that. We just scrape by. Have to go into debt a lot to do it."

"With what we draw we can't buy no new clothes," a voice said from the darkness. It belonged to Mrs. Jackson, a quiet, light-complexioned woman in her mid-thirties, about 20 years younger than her husband. She wore a worn sweater and faded red levis.

"If it weren't for our family helping out I don't know what we'd do," she said. "All's I have to wear is what my sister sends me."

The Jacksons and their two daughters—Kathy, 8, and Vickey, 4—live on Ice House Creek, near Manchester, in what Toleman describes as "the coldest house in the United States." It is a four-room frame structure with a lean-to kitchen, a big house by the standards of the Appalachian poor. The outside is covered with freshly painted white siding. A few chickens wander about the well-kept yard. Inside there is no insulation to keep out the cold, not even wallboard to slow it down.

The temperature was 20 degrees outside. Inside, the fire

had been ablaze for hours. Nonetheless, Jackson wore a heavy gray carcoat with the threads worn bare at the cuffs. He hadn't worked in seven years, ever since his car careened off an Indiana highway. He suffered a slipped disc and internal injuries in the crash and was hospitalized for months.

Prior to the accident he worked as a machine-press operator in Indiana and made "big money." For three years now he had tried unsuccessfully to get Social Security disability benefits. Five doctors had attested to his disability, but his case was still waiting appeal in federal court. He isn't sure why. He doesn't understand the complexities of "justice," why it works for the Mafia and the rich but not for the poor. Secretly, he thinks there is some logic to it that he can't grasp simply because "I ain't got no education."

"To tell the truth," Jackson said, "sometimes I can set right down and write my name good as any man just like that. Then again I sit there and nothing comes. It's my nerves."

The Jacksons are almost total wards of the welfare state. Their $150 check comes from the state Department of Public Assistance. Their children receive free lunch at school. And the family would probably starve if it weren't for food stamps. They pay $42 for $106 worth of stamps every month that they can afford it—about three-fourths of the time.

The only place the Jacksons, and scores of other families like them in Clay County, can look for any improvement in their lives is to the federal government. But Toleman doesn't put much stock in "them fellas up in Washington."

"Here's what I can't see out," he said. "President Nixon a few months back he asked fer—imagine they give it to him by now—anyway, he asked fer $550 million to give to Cambodia. Them Cambodians they already torn their own country up and killed our boys. Now they want us to give 'em money. If they'd turn that same money loose to every poor person and let them put up a good house you wouldn't have any poor people after awhile."

Toleman stared into the fire for about two minutes, then added:

"If those politicians and rich folks would do some home visitin' they'd think a lot different."

Robert Hensley

He was working. His job as bus driver for the local Head Start program wasn't much. It paid only $1.65 a hour, but it had helped him buy a new pickup and keep his eight children off the welfare rolls. He was at the wheel of his bus, bouncing down a rocky creek bed, when he told me that people in Clay County had changed in recent years.

"Used to be people would holler when they walked past. Maybe sit and talk awhile. That don't happen no more. Now you pass them on the street they wouldn't even raise their heads. People you've knowed for years won't talk to you.

"Even three years back people would come by my house and eat and talk and stay half the night," he continued. "Now I haven't had anyone but my brother drop by in over a year. Had three hogs and I couldn't even hire anyone to help kill 'em. Used to be half the hollow would help you render a hog, then sit up all night and help you eat it."

Hensley, a short, matter-of-fact man of about 55, wasn't sure what provoked the change. Part, he thought, was welfare, part people moving away to work for factories, part something no one could put his finger on. But whatever it was, the change had Hensley and many mountaineers like him worried.

"It's gotten so you can't even get enough men to dig a grave," he said. "Used to be you'd never have no trouble rounding up volunteers to dig a grave."

11

The Rich Hillbillies

Ed Venters is the most forgotten of all hillbillies. He gets mad about it every time he picks up the morning newspaper. It comes from Louisville, 210 miles away from his home in Pikeville, Kentucky. Almost every day there's something about eastern Kentucky in it that he doesn't like. Headlines about children going hungry, coal mines killing their fathers and schools that don't teach anyone how to read.

Venters seldom gets beyond the headlines. He has seen them all before. Usually he'll toss the paper down in disgust. The press lies. And if Venters didn't know it to be true himself, someone would surely remind him of it at the Green Meadows Country Club.

"The newspapers make us look like dirty clods," he declares. "People would be damned surprised if they knew what things are really like here."

135

Venters knows all about what "things are really like" in Appalachia, particularly that part around Pikeville, Kentucky, in the heart of the poverty belt, where he has spent most of his life.

"I'm a hillbilly," he says. "Deep down in my heart I'm just a typical ole hillbilly."

Venters owns Childers and Venters, Inc., in Pikeville. He sells Cadillacs. And he is probably the only "typical ole hillbilly" in the world to sell 25 Cadillacs—Fleetwoods, Coupe de Villes, El Dorados, some with price tags in the $11,000 range—and 75 Pontiacs last year.

His per capita sales—equivalent to 2,000 Cadillacs in a market the size of Louisville—would make him the envy of any car salesman in the country. But Venters doesn't worry about per capita figures. He is more concerned about his high-priced competition. "The Continentals are breaking into the Pikeville field real strong," explained one woman in the country-club set. "You can see we like our cars big and cushy."

Luxury autos aren't uncommon on the streets of most mountain county-seat towns. But Pikeville has more than its share of Cadillacs, Lincolns, Imperials and Buicks. It has more than its share of "rich hillbillies."

The "good livers," as they are called by their less affluent neighbors, take no offense at being called "hillbillies." That's just something anyone who grows up in an area surrounded by hills is called. They know they live pretty much the same as—or even better than—their silk-stocking counterparts in Lake Forest, Scarsdale or Bel Air. They travel to the same Florida winter retreats; they send their offspring to the same Eastern universities; they read the same fashion ads in *Vogue*; they drive the same plush autos and they study the same stock quotations in *The Wall Street Journal*.

What they don't like is the picture everyone has of their home area. It hurts their pride, their sense of fair play, their social life away from home and sometimes even their business. As one wealthy matron put it, "Every time you go somewhere people ask if we really go barefoot at home, or if we still have moonshine stills in our backyards." As this woman, and most other rich hillbillies, see it, Pikeville isn't a poverty mecca, but a booming community of 4,700 with 50–75 millionaires, 35 lawyers, 25 doctors, 20 swimming pools, a new $7-million hospital, 3 banks with deposits totaling more than $100 million, a country club "as snobby as they come," prospects for a beginning doctor to earn $30,000 to $50,000 his first year in practice.

Hardly a place to go hungry, hardly the setting for a mountain feud, Pikeville is a secure place to make a buck, a secure place to spend it, to sip Kentucky bourbon and boast what a good place Pikeville is to grow old and rich in—far from the wicked big cities, the blacks ("We never have any trouble from our coloreds"), commie liberals, high taxes, sex education, junkies, hippie freaks and peace demonstrators. These are city problems. Pike County doesn't have them. It's patriotic, very patriotic. It doesn't court outsiders or strange ideas. When *Look* magazine came out with a special issue in 1968 commemorating the 50th anniversary of the Bolshevik revolution, it was barred from Pikeville newstands. You can't be too careful, one clerk told me. Rich hillbillies can feel secure in Pikeville. Their values are intact. The only problem is the image.

Meet Henry David Stratton, lawyer, civic booster, coal operator, former country-club president, and behind-the-scenes mover in much that happens in Pikeville, Kentucky.

"Everyone has a Li'l Abner view of us. They think we all

live in a log cabin in some hollow," he was saying. "It hurts us economically. No industry wants to move into a place that sounds like that. Some insurance companies won't even write policies here."

Stratton lives in a new $100,000 home beside the Big Sandy River. His law firm occupies most of the second floor of the Ward Building in downtown Pikeville. He is tall and courtly, and anything but poor.

"Our image is the real problem. It's gotten worse with so much emphasis on poverty the last few years," he said. "And of course, the coal industry has always been a whipping boy.

"You talk to someone outside the region and they won't listen to you. You try to tell a doctor you want to recruit about our All-American City award, or our college, or our new hospital and all they see in their minds is an old weather-beaten shack. So we're facing a critical doctor shortage. Same thing with lawyers. It's too bad. We all have more business than we can handle. There's money to be made here."

Where does the money come from?

Coal.

Who has it?

"The coal people and everyone they do business with—the doctors, the lawyers, the merchants, everyone," said Walter P. Walters, of the Walter P. Walters Insurance Agency.

His new bronze-and-black Lincoln Continental had just swung into Bowles Addition, Pikeville's classiest subdivision.

"When someone hears 'Pikeville,' they say, 'That's up in the poverty area. They picture us carrying moonshine jugs and leading hound dogs around like some ignoramus mountaineers," said Walters.

Bowles Addition sits in the flat bottom land on the north side of town, tucked in a bend in the Big Sandy River. Its sprawling brick ranch houses, ranging in value from $35,000 to $200,000, are about as far from poverty as you can get. Walters, snowy haired and erect, wanted to make sure I understood what put them there.

"Our economy depends entirely on coal," he said. "When the coal business is good everyone's business is good. It spreads out all over town." The previous year had been a good year for coal. It had been a good year for Walters. He sold insurance carrying more than $1 million in premiums.

"You can see the money in the houses," he said. "That one belongs to an attorney, the one next to it to an oil and gas distributor. The big one over there—that's Tom Ratliff's, he's in the coal business. This fellow is an electrical contractor. That new one is Henry Stratton's. It'll go for at least $100,000."

And so it went down one block and up the next and down the next. Past swimming pools. Past perhaps 20 Cadillacs. The 1970 census found that one home in three in Pike County didn't have indoor plumbing. Those homes were far away in places like Poorbottom Hollow or Wolf Pit or Lower Pompey. Places few rich hillbillies ever visit. Places some doubt even exist.

"Look at that one," Walters continued as his big car wheeled down a long, tree-shaded lane. At the end of the lane was a handsome colonial mansion. In the garage were a speedboat and a huge houseboat. In the back yard rested a helicopter belonging to the owner of the house, Stuart Adams, a contractor.

"Now, if they do away with the coal business like they're trying to do with this mine-safety law, they'll do away with prosperity here. Those loudmouths who are always getting their names in the papers don't understand what coal means to us. They don't understand what it's like here."

Dr. Thomas H. Johns, the tenth president of Pikeville College, didn't understand the rich hillbillies. He didn't understand red-baiting; he didn't understand the power of the coal interests; and he didn't understand the grip the rich had on politics in the region. When he found out about them, he vowed, "I'm not going to sell my soul for prejudice, hate or bigotry." Dr. Thomas H. Johns lasted two years as president of Pikeville College.

The college, dug into the mountain slope above Pikeville, was on hard days when Johns arrived in 1967. It had just lost its ninth president in a flurry of rumors and was known in academic circles as a "sleepy hollow" operation in danger of losing its accreditation. Its endowment was almost nonexistent; support from the Presbyterian Church, which founded the institution, appeared on the wane. Johns, young and crusade-minded, seemed the ideal candidate to change it. At 36, he was an ordained minister and a former college Little All-American football tackle. He had a Ph.D. and experience as an administrator at three colleges behind him.

Once at Pikeville, Johns moved fast—too fast, it turned out. He hired 30 new teachers, appointed students to trustee committees, put in a new curriculum with emphasis on sociology and psychology, encouraged students to speak out on social problems and urged them to "do your own thing." This all might have made him a campus darling at Berkeley or Columbia—but not at Pikeville, where students were still asked as freshmen to sign a pledge that they wouldn't drink alcoholic beverages during their college careers. "We don't know what our thing is," complained one coed. "And even if we did, we wouldn't know how to do it."

At a time when radical students across the nation were rebelling against conservative administrators, Johns suddenly found himself in an inconceivable situation—conservative students were accusing him of being too radical. They complained about their classes being too freewheeling, the alleged leftist leanings of the long-haired male professors and the miniskirts worn by their female professors.

"We must have the only right-wing student protest movement in the country," boasted one conservative senior. One student group considered impeachment proceedings. Another started a vicious whisper campaign. Soon the entire community was at odds with the young president. Campus radicals were stunned. "We're a minority," said one transfer student from Syracuse University. "We've been grossed out."

Johns argued that the controversy was good. "Peaches and cream don't bring dialogue, but confrontation does," he said. "Polarization of ideas is what education is all about—it makes people aware of their own thinking."

The college's board of trustees, though packed with conservative Pikeville businessmen, originally supported Johns. And had it not been for two fatal mistakes he perhaps would be their college president today. One was his wife, a fiery Iowa farm girl. She felt that her afternoons were better spent teaching sewing at a controversial antipoverty center than playing bridge with the town's female elite. The other was the college's newfound interest in strip mining and the problems of the poor. This interest led Johns to sponsor a strip-mining symposium and join a number of other Appalachian colleges in a low-key antipoverty effort.

These actions bordered on heresy to most rich hillbillies, many of whom had acquired their riches either by exploiting the poor or by going into the strip-mining business. They struck back. Robert Holcomb, president of the local Chamber of Commerce and a well-known strip-mine spokesman, led the onslaught. First, unsigned leaflets circulated the area, implying that one of Johns' new faculty members had "communist leanings." Next came two investigations. The first was a local affair conducted by a special trustee committee. The second was a witch-hunt by the fledging Kentucky Committee on Un-American Activities (KUAC), which came to the county at Holcomb's request.

Five months after KUAC's last hearing, what Johns described as "a small majority" of Pikeville trustees pressured him to resign.

"True men must always assume risks," he told a campus gathering that night. "The students at Pikeville who have been set free have no intention of being enslaved by bigotry, hate or disenfranchisement by political manipulation."

Two days later the Pikeville Student Government Association demanded that all trustees living in a three-county area resign because their economic and political interests made it impossible for them to serve the college. "We're concerned that the same thing that happened to Dr. Johns may happen to his successor if he tries to do anything but play lap dog to the local power structure," said student president Charles E. Moore.

None of the rich hillbillies on the board resigned.

Pikeville, like most mountain towns, has always had a strong, largely self-perpetuating upper middle class, Robert B. Johnson, president of Pikeville National Bank, was saying.

"We haven't had the extremely wealthy people in the $50–$100 million class," he said. "But we do have a great number of people who are well-to-do."

Bruce Walters, who owns the local Ford agency, is one of them. Johnson was in Walters' sunken living room, beside the big glass doors opening onto the patio that leads to the swimming pool where six smallmouth bass were swimming.

Walters was out of town, but the banker was conducting a guided tour of his luxurious home.

"That's the kind of neighbors we have here. This is one of the few places you can go to bed at night without locking your doors," Johnson said.

He offered me a martini, opening a liquor cabinet containing 11 bottles of Beefeater gin.

"Liquor supply's down," he said. "Rather have a beer?"

The beer was in a refrigerated keg. It tasted good. We moved onto the patio across from the balcony leading to Walters' second-floor bedroom. The balcony is called "Pauper's Perch," apparently in honor of the 52 percent of Pike County's residents who live on annual incomes of less than $3,200.

"We don't have the isolated rich here that you do in the city," Johnson said. "You have a party here and you'll invite the guy who works on your car at the gas station as soon as you'll invite some lawyer or doctor. You don't look at someone's background or finances. If someone's your friend, they're your friend."

The Johnson's ranch house was less than two blocks away. The banker's attractive wife, Bryan, was lounging beside the swimming pool. Her skin was a deep brown. She had just returned from a month in Florida. I asked her about poor people.

"We have indigent people like everyplace else, and some of them need help," she said. "But we don't have any more than anyplace else despite what you read in *Life* or *Look* magazine."

Bryan Johnson is a transplanted hillbilly who is proud of the title "hillbilly." She's sold on the region and believes mountain people "don't have that class system people have some other places." She is relieved that Pike County has never had "any trouble with our coloreds," that the blacks have had the good sense never to demonstrate.

Her husband nodded in agreement. "There are more patriots in eastern Kentucky than anywhere in the United States," he said. "You get some hippies, or yippies, parading on the streets wearing American flags or waving something about the Viet Cong, they won't get along in Pikeville. Someone would run them out."

There is a precedent, of sorts. It happened in 1967-68 during the heyday of the War on Poverty. With all the world to choose from, the political leaders of Pike County, Kentucky, concluded that the international communist menace had decided to overthrow their local government.

Why Pike County? I asked a wealthy young businessman during the height of the "revolution."

"Why not," he said. "They have to start somewhere. Pike County is as good as anyplace else. After all, we're the largest coal-producing county in the country."

The so-called communist menace consisted of three rather ineffectual antipoverty workers who lived in an old farmhouse near Pikeville: Alan McSurely, a 30-year-old Washingtonian with a master's degree in psychology, his wife Margaret, who had worked for the Student Nonviolent Coordinating Committee during the Mississippi Summer of 1964, and Joseph Mulloy, the son of a Louisville plumber.

The threesome's first crime against the Pike County government was that they went to work for unpopular employers. At the time the "conspiracy" arose, Mulloy was employed by the Appalachian Volunteers, a federally funded antipoverty group. McSurely had originally come to the mountains to work with the same organization but was fired for manipulative tactics after three weeks on the job. He and his wife were soon hired by the Southern Conference Educational Fund (SCEF), a civil-rights group making its first thrust into Appalachia.

They entered a hotbed of suspicion. The Appalachian Volunteers, or AV's, as they were called, pictured themselves as the commandos in the poverty effort, choosing as their battleground the most isolated of hollows where the poorest of the poor lived. By the time Mulloy and the McSureleys arrived in Pike County, the AV's, who had already been the subject of at least three dozen editorials in small-town newspapers, were being berated for everything from their politics to their clothes. And for every person who had ever read an editorial or seen a real live AV in the flesh, a hundred more had been frightened silly by vicious rumors. To listen to the idle gossip in those months, one might have pictured the AV's as the baddest, dirtiest, shaggiest, most sex-crazed, leftist weirdos in all of Christendom—a sort of Hell's Angels with a social conscience.

Most of it was untrue, of course. But the fact that the daughter of a former Kentucky governor and some of the most concerned and idealistic students the state had ever produced were spending months doing such mundane tasks as painting one-room schoolhouses didn't deter the critics. The SCEF was even more suspect. It had long been a target of right-wing legislatures in the South, and its executive director had once been convicted of "founding a two-member communist cell with a female FBI agent," a charge later thrown out by an appeals court.

Red-baiting was nothing new to the eastern Kentucky mountains. Coal operators had used it for decades to scare their employes away from the union organizers. And one of the reasons that the United Mine Workers succeeded where other unions failed was that John L. Lewis was able to cloak himself in a robe of anticommunism. Pike County—in the form of Chamber of Commerce president Robert Holcomb and commonwealth attorney Thomas Ratliff—brought a special zeal to the task, however.

It began one night late in July, 1967, when Holcomb and the Pike County sheriff visited the McSurely-Mulloy farmhouse. They stayed an hour, chatting with Mulloy. Their exact purpose was unclear. One ready answer is that the AV's and SCEF were in the midst of an anti-strip-mining campaign and Holcomb, president of the National Indepen-dent Coal Operators Association, was upset. That night he called for a federal investigation of AV activities.

On August 12, Ratliff, a Republican candidate for lieu-tenant-governor, and 12 armed deputies invaded the farmhouse just after midnight. They seized two truckloads of reading material—including *The Essential Works of Lenin*, *The Poems of Chairman Mao*, *The Quotations of Mao Tse-tung* and *Catch-22*—and charged Mulloy and the two Mc-Surelys with sedition against the United States and the Com-monwealth of Kentucky.

"We know that these people are communists," Holcomb told reporters. "There are no ifs, ands or buts about it . . . they intend to take over the county."

Ratliff promptly convinced the county grand jury of the same. It indicted the trio, along with SCEF executive director Carl Braden and his wife, for sedition. The grand jury report said a "well organized and well financed effort is being made to promote and spread the Communist theory . . . to overthrow the government of Pike County."

One month later a U.S. District Court panel declared Ken-tucky's 46-year-old sedition law unconstitutional, ordered siezed materials returned and enjoined Pike County officials from taking any further action against the five.

But the damage was done. The McSurelys left the county after a night rider threw a bomb through their bedroom window. It took them more than three years to free themselves from the legal web that started with a midnight knock on their door. In October, 1970, Alan was sentenced to a year in prison and Margaret to three months for contempt of Congress after they refused to turn over materials seized in the raid to a Senate committee investigating urban riots.

Mulloy was drafted in 1968 by the same selective service board that drafted fellow Louisvillian Muhummed Ali. He didn't return to the mountains permanently until the Supreme Court ordered the board to rehear his conscientious-objector plea.

The AV's, which fired Mulloy after he refused the draft, survived almost two years after the sedition raid, their federal funds first drastically reduced and then eliminated. The death blow came in November, 1968, when KUAC declared, after a two-day hearing, that the AV's were a "tremendous detriment to the deserving people of this region." The organization was too weak to fight back except through press releases. When KUAC returned to the county two months later only one AV, Mrs. Edith Easterling, 43, a lifelong Pike County resident, testified. She told of a continual pattern of official and unofficial harassment, including telephoned threats and shots fired through the windows of her home, since she opened an AV outpost, called the Marrowbone Folk School, near her home.

"I'm proud of the AV's and proud to be a Pike Countian," she said. "But I confess that I have done wrong. I voted for that dirty bunch down in the Courthouse."

The AV's died out six months later.

The rich hillbillies survived. Coal boomed. Some rich operators, like Thomas Ratliff, got richer. A few poor operators got rich for the first time, creating a new round of Horatio Alger stories. Bank deposits mushroomed. Those of Pikeville National Bank & Trust grew $20 million during 1970 alone. *Playboy, Vogue* and *Cosmopolitan* climbed to the best-seller lists on local newstands.

Coal had again proved itself king. The rich hillbillies felt secure. And as they tell about it, they are convincing. They are likable people, gracious to visitors, thoughtful in personal relationships, people little different from their affluent counterparts in most of "middle America." They are proud people who want visitors to approve of their life.

Mrs. Oscar Sowards is one of the best. Her husband makes his money by financing apartment projects. She is a former president of the Kentucky Federation of Women's Clubs, chairman of the Kentucky Citizens Commission on Consumer Protection and creator of a program to help the poor stretch their consumer dollars.

"This is a place where the American dream still works," she was saying. The coal boom had proved that. Half a dozen or more local boys in their late twenties and early thirties had become millionaires because of it.

"We have a proud people who believe in democracy," she said. "These are all home-grown boys who have stayed and proved the economy in this part of the country is good."

The Sowards have lived in Pikeville since they were married 32 years ago. For a quarter-century they kept a winter house in Florida, but they gave that up. Later they thought about moving. It would be more convenient for Oscar's business and his wife's civic activities.

"We could sell our house here anytime we want to for $75,000 and move on to Lexington or somewhere. But we like it here," Mrs. Sowards said.

"We feel this is the greatest place in the world; its people are the finest on earth."

The Sowards, like many rich hillbillies, have seen much of the world. They have been around it three times. They had just returned from their second cruise to South America. But they are always eager to return home.

"We have everything here you could ever want," Mrs. Sowards said. "And if I'm somewhere and someone asks me where I'm from, I'm proud to say, 'Oh, I'm just an ol' Kentucky hillbilly.' "

12

The Strippers

Mrs. Ruby Caudill was alone in her place on Johnnie Collins Hollow when the mountain came rolling down the hill. Her husband, Burt, was "off workin' in the mines." She was watching television. The sun had dropped below the mountain three hours before.

"It came roarin' down the hill with a sound I ain't ever heard before," she said. "I tell you I was plumb scared. You couldn't see nothin'.

"Then the neighbors came knockin' at my door and told me the mountain had slid down. They took me away because we was afraid what would happen."

Burt Caudill returned home hours later. He found that a 200-yard-long pile of earth and debris 12 feet high had slid down the mountainside to within 50 yards of his house. Trees, some with trunks more than 20 inches in diameter, had been uprooted, boulders dislodged, mud, dirt and rocks stacked high, bushes erased, his pasture land destroyed.

"If it weren't for that bend up there it would have taken the house too," he said later, climbing atop the ruin. "I've got my life invested in this place."

"I never asked them to come and do this to my land. The state gave them permission. I don't believe they should take a man's land like this. It's just like renting if they do."

The disaster visited upon the Caudills is called strip mining. It is an entirely legal—and, in fact, state-sanctioned— practice of gouging rich seams of coal from mountainsides. Burt Caudill had no particular feelings of outrage about it six months before, when the Valley Coal Company, of Whitesburg, Kentucky, brought its bulldozers to Johnnie Collins Hollow to peel off the surface of the mountain above his place. He has been a coal miner all his life and by his reckoning, "The coal's made here to git."

But before long silt began washing into the creek that bubbles down the hollow. Later a boulder crashed down into a hog shed on William Sexton's place, a quarter-mile away. About that time Burt Caudill climbed the mountain behind his house to talk with Victor Hurley, the mine operator. He told him he thought Hurley's bulldozers were pushing dirt on his land needlessly. Hurley disagreed but promised to do better. Caudill next went to his lawyer. "He said weren't nothing we could do," he recalled.

Caudill is a lean, sandy-haired man of about 50 with a balloonlike nose. He bought his house and the 10 acres around the mouth of the hollow 13 years ago. He remodeled the house, put carpet on the floors and wood paneling on the living-room walls. And he worked the land, hauled away brush, repaired the shed.

"Everything I got is right here," he said. "My life's savings. My life's work."

He pointed to a spot three-fourths of the way up the hill where an earlier slide had ripped through his barbed-wire fence.

"From there on up ain't no use to me no more. Can't use it for pasture, that's for sure. Used to graze stock all over here. Got rid of them after they started stripping. Couldn't get nothing for 'em. Almost had to give 'em away. I kept hearing something breaking and cracking. Knew something was going to happen."

Caudill is a deep miner. A quarter of a century ago when mining was a matter of men going underground and digging, almost all Kentucky miners were deep miners. Now gigantic earth-moving machines, huge augers and King-Kong-like scoop shovels mine 37 percent of the nation's coal, scraping and ripping it from the surface. These strip miners have left a legacy of destruction in Johnnie Collins Hollow and much of Appalachia. Their bulldozers have cut ugly contour strips in rings around mountaintops, dumping tons of "overburden," or waste, down the sides of mountains. Trees have been uprooted and buried. Homes destroyed. Hills laid bare. Game and wildlife driven from their habitats. Streams clogged with silt and acid. More than 3 million acres, roughly the area of Connecticut, have already been ravaged. Much of the land has been left unfit for human inhabitation or use, and the pace of strip mining increases each year. In addition, an estimated 10,500 miles of once-clear Appalachian streams have been contaminated. The U.S. Department of the Interior has said it would take at least $250 million to reclaim the ruin. Yet little has been done to start such an effort.

The human waste and suffering can't be measured so conveniently. Years ago unsuspecting mountain farmers sold the mineral rights to their land to transient land agents for a pittance—usually 50 cents an acre. The "long deeds"—sometimes called broadform deeds—gave the holder a claim to any minerals under the surface.

To the mountaineer it seemed a sensible enough move, for he knew of no minerals under his pastures. But in the early 1900's the children of these farmers discovered that their parents had sold away the right to rich seams of coal and great pools of oil. In the 1950's and 1960's, the descendants of those same illiterate farmers discovered that the long deeds also gave the holder the right to bulldoze any building, or field, or stand of timber that covered the coal. Dozens of them awoke mornings to find bulldozers ripping at the mountainsides above their homes, often destroying their pasture land and gardens and sending tons of debris toward their homes. In short order, their crops were ruined. Their once-pleasant valleys were turned into painful eyesores. Gaunt, silent mountaineers suddenly rose up in anger. A few bulldozers were dynamited. Gunshots were fired. One widow planted herself in front of a coal-company bulldozer, daring it to trespass on her land. Here and there farmers gave up their traditional isolation to join groups fighting coal interests. But mostly the mountaineer brooded in lonely agony.

Kentucky, Pennsylvania and West Virginia passed "tough" strip-mine-control laws in apparent recognition of this anger. Coal operators, long prophets of doom, predicted the new regulations would destroy the industry and throw hundreds of miners out of work. They didn't. The coal industry continued to prosper. Strip mining, because it is almost twice as productive per man-day as underground mining, grew even faster than the rest of the industry. In Kentucky alone, the number of licensed strip-mine operators increased twofold between 1966 and 1971. The largest single increase, a harbinger of things to come, came between January and December, 1970, when 168 new strip miners obtained mining permits. Some of their number were conscientious businessmen, who made honest attempts to reclaim the land they uprooted. But many, according to one of the state's top reclamation officials, "were outlaws and scallawags out for a quick buck."

Most strip miners, the good and the bad, operate alike. First their agile bulldozers slice deep, right-angle notches into the side of the mountain above the seam of coal they plan to extract, much as if they were excavating for a mountain road. Any trees or plant life that lie in their path are shoveled down the hillside, later to be covered with tons of shattered shale and sterile subsoil of clay and rock. All vegetation, often for hundreds of feet, is buried in the piles of debris—aptly called spoil banks. A sheer, barren highwall is left on one side of the notch as the bulldozers chew their way downward. When they strike solid bedrock, giant drilling rigs bore six-inch holes through the rock to the coal seams below. Miners then fill the holes with a makeshift explosive. The blast pitches broken bits of shale and dirt high in the air. The mountain heaves. The bedrock bulges, then cracks into hundreds of pieces. When they are removed, a bare seam of coal remains. It is easily stripped from its resting place and loaded into 40-ton trucks for the trip down the mountainside to waiting rail cars miles away.

The bulldozers continue eating their way across the ridge, often for miles. Each mountain contains several major coal seams, and when the 'dozers have encircled the entire mountain, stripping the coal at one ridge level, they will sometimes move to a higher level and start the same process over again. But even under the best of circumstances, they can remove only a small portion of the outside rim of the coal seam, leaving the vast bulk of it undisturbed.

It is economically impractical to remove the remaining coal by stripping. The coal auger was developed to get some of it. Originally, the auger, a gigantic drill, was employed after a ridge had been strip mined. It was placed against the highwall, and its bits, sometimes as large as seven feet in diameter, bored into the mountainside. With extensions, the drill could reach as far as 70 yards into the heart of the mountain, spewing large quantities of coal to the surface. Once one borehole was completed, the auger was removed and another hole started a few inches or feet away. The process is extremely wasteful, for it removes only about 50 percent of the coal although it makes further extraction impossible. But it is an extremely profitable method—so profitable that augers now attack virgin lands as well as strip-mine sites.

Until recent years, strip and auger mining were largely unregulated in Kentucky and most of central Appalachia. Control laws were weak and only sporadically enforced. As late as 1964, Kentucky employed only four inspectors to oversee strip mines. Even if the state had had adequate regulations, the commitment to enforcement would have been too small to expect meaningful results. And when enforcement officers did try to exercise reasonable controls, they found themselves in knockdown, dragout fights with operators, with the courts almost always deciding in favor of the operators. Today, the thousands of acres of once-beautiful hillsides stripped bare during those reckless years remain festering sores on the landscape, their strip-mine benches cutting into the hillsides like ugly notches on a gunslinger's pistol, their spoil banks spilling down into the valleys. In Kentucky alone, 100,000 acres await reclamation, bitter reminders that, as east Kentuckians say, "You can't put a mountain back together."

Relatively little has been done to try to reclaim the land. Kentucky's 1966 strip-mine control law failed to offer any provisions or money to reclaim abandoned strip-mine land. It did, however, place strong enforcement and regulatory powers in the hands of the Director of Strip Mine Reclamation, including authority to set minimum standards to prevent stream pollution, assure revegetation and repair damaged landscapes. The law has improved reclamation fivefold, leaching the criticism of strip-mine practices and forcing strip miners to develop new techniques to prevent erosion and acid runoff.

But severe problems remain.

Burt and Ruby Caudill know about one of them—earthslides. The heavy December and January rains sent five slides crashing down the hillsides of Johnnie Collins Hollow. The one on their property was the largest and most destructive, but two other homes also were threatened. As a result, the state Division of Reclamation closed down Valley Coal Company's strip mine for a week and ordered it to "clean up the mess" and move its operations to a less heavily populated area. Company bulldozers did "clean up the mess," but only after an insurance agent told Mrs. Caudill that the slides were "an act of God" and that the strip miners had no control over them.

A 1969 U.S. Forestry Service report disclosed another problem. After a lengthy study of runoff and erosion in three watershed areas near strip mines in Quicksand, Kentucky, it concluded that new grading and drainage regulations designed to save streams were not working. Creeks near strip mines were found to have just as much siltation as existed before the 1966 law. Streams were filling up with mud; those below strip mines were found to contain 15 times more sediment than those in nonstripped areas. Aquatic life had been killed off or driven downstream to cleaner waters. Fish at three of six measuring stations in one hollow had all but disappeared. Mayflies, one of the basic foods of young fish, showed a 90 percent decline during the study period. Creek chubs, stonerollers, shiners and other minnows had moved to other waters. An Eastern Kentucky University natural-science instructor who took part in the research told how he had found one full-grown salamander entombed by silt: "I picked up a rock and found this dead salamander. It was like finding a fossil that was made yesterday. This indicates the tremendous amount of silt that will come pouring down during a heavy rain—enough to trap a highly mobile salamander."

What can be done? In its most comprehensive statement to date on the subject, the U.S. Department of the Interior in 1967 said:

> Elementary principles of resource management dictate that our nation put a stop to unnecessary damage from future mining, and begin an orderly program to repair damage from past mining. . . . If the efforts of state and local government and private enterprises continue to fall short, the new federal programs also should be designed to assume without delay a large measure of direct federal action.

The report recommended a stiff regulatory approach to strip mining. Many conservationists would prefer an out-and-out ban on strip-mine activities, particularly in mountain areas. West Virginia Congressman Ken Hechler and 16 other lawmakers introduced such measures in the 92nd Congress. A scaled-down ban, prohibiting strip mining in 32 West Virginia counties, won a partial victory in the 1971 legislature, and the subject will doubtlessly come up whenever Appalachian conservationists and lawmakers gather for the next decade.

The Stripper

At 46, William B. Sturgill wears the title of Kentucky's most hated strip miner with quiet dignity. His drawl is flat and smooth; his manner, easygoing. He carries his portly 200 pounds with the agility of a former athlete (he starred on the University of Kentucky's 1946 Southeastern Conference championship basketball team) and the assurance of a small-town millionaire. He is equally comfortable in a Brooks Brothers suit and buttondown shirt at the governor's mansion in Frankfort and in quilted ski jacket and khaki trousers on the slopes of one of the hills his bulldozers have ravaged. He calls it "surface mining"—the term has a less damning ring than "strip mining." And for him, "The question is not whether we're going to have surface mining, but how we're going to reclaim surface-mined land."

Sturgill has spent thousands of dollars developing new mining techniques and showcase reclamation sites to display to visiting politicians and journalists in an attempt to convince them that strip mining is a constructive, not a destructive, industry. His arguments are familiar. The nation needs coal. Coal produces 56 percent of the country's electrical power and is vital to dozens of other industries. Strip mining is the easiest, cheapest and safest way to dig it. Furthermore, in a poverty-scarred region like Appalachia, strip mining provides jobs and cash for mine operators, mine workers, truck drivers, railroads and utility companies.

Until recently, Bill Sturgill was the biggest strip miner in the Hazard, Kentucky, coalfield. As such, he is held in high regard among the businessmen of the area. He has given tirelessly of his time for civic projects, they'll tell you, emceed countless luncheon gatherings and raised money for such respectable "safe" social agencies as the Red Cross. (He despises more activist groups and insists that hundreds of mountaineers are on welfare simply because they're "too sorry" to work.) His political influence helped the town get a two-year community college, and he has been named one of six "outstanding" Kentuckians for his civic work. "You won't find a better citizen," says one banker. "I'm proud to call him my friend."

A visit to Hardburly, Clear Creek, Cordia, Lotts Creek or a dozen other isolated hollows and half-deserted coaltowns uncovers a quite different view of Bill Sturgill. Here the mere mention of his name kindles red-faced rage and brings forth tales of his bulldozers' uprooting the coffins of infants, needlessly pillaging the hillsides and pushing tons of mud and rock toward the homes of ailing widows. Paul Ashley, a schoolteacher who lives on Clear Creek in Knott County, Kentucky, spoke for many when he said:

"When he's finished with something it looks like the Arizona desert. It's hard for anyone who hasn't seen it to imagine how bad he leaves the land. He's destroyed our mountains, he's destroyed our timber and our streams, and his coal trucks have ruined our roads."

For 12 years, Bill Sturgill was co-owner of Kentucky Oaks Coal Company and a series of subsidiaries. He strip mined more coal than any other independent coal operator in Kentucky and, in the process, desecrated more of the state's landscape than any single man in its history. He defends his action on economic grounds. "The beauty of the mountains provides nothing to the economic life of their residents," he told one interviewer. "They must rely on coal, and hardly anything else."

Sturgill relied on coal and the broad form deed to earn his riches. "I never liked it," he says. "I used the broad form deed and made money off it, because it was legal—and still is, the courts have upheld it 13 times now—and because that's what we had to work with." To his credit, Sturgill normally paid landowners a nominal fee for ramrodding onto their land.

Usually the mountaineers would take his dollars in somber silence, and the bulldozers would move in. But in November, 1965, Mrs. Ollie "Widow" Combs, of Honey Gap, Kentucky, refused to move. When the bulldozers rumbled across the ridge she threw herself in their path. "We live hard," Mrs. Combs, a frail wisp of a woman, told a bulldozer driver. "I don't bother anyone, but you come into our homes. I just want to live out my life in my hollow and be left alone." She was arrested, but she returned the next day, climbing the winding path to where the bulldozers would come. Again she sat down in front of the blade of the big yellow bulldozer and again the law came. The lawmen picked her up and carried her down the mountain to a police car. Two months later the lonely widow who had defied the law and the coal boss begged the Kentucky legislature to "stop them from destroying what people got . . . destroying their homes and their land and their children." The lawmakers listened attentively. A few weeks later they passed what was then described as the nation's toughest anti-strip-mine law.

Sturgill hovered in the Senate gallery as the legislators voted. "I thought it was a bad, unnecessary law, and I fought it enthusiastically, just as I have supported it and urged others to support it since it was passed," he says.

"We always have wanted to be good citizens," he told a newsman at the time of the Widow Combs incident. "We are proud of our record and we are proud of our diligent efforts to support the economy of this area."

Sturgill's record as a "good citizen" under the new mining law is a questionable one. His strip mines have been praised as some of Kentucky's best reclamation efforts. Yet they also had some of the state's worst landslides. Publicly, Sturgill has adamantly supported the law. Yet his own mines have been cited six times—more than those of any other single operator —for violating the law.

"No, I have no apologies for surface mining," he says. "The country has to have energy and we have more coal than any other fuel. Economics dictate that it be produced as cheaply as possible, and in many cases this means by strip mining."

In the fall of 1970, Bill Sturgill and his long-time partner Richard Kelly sold out their strip-mining interests for $10.5 million. A few months later, Sturgill officially retired, at least temporarily, from the business. "Of course, I will continue my interest in public affairs," he said. "I have always been interested in public issues."

The Enforcers

"Strip mining has been an ugly thing and it'll continue to be ugly as long as operators ignore the law," Bill Hayes was saying at his desk in the Division of Strip Mining and Reclamation office in Hazard, Kentucky. He had just ushered a strip-mine operator out the door. The operator had wanted Hayes to issue him a permit to strip coal from a ridge above 15 homes. Hayes had asked what would happen to the people who lived in the houses. The mine operator had replied, "They don't matter. Kentucky River [a landholding company] owns them all. They'll move 'em out if I get too close."

Hayes was still shaking his head five minutes later. "That's the way it is every day," he said. "Someone coming in here like that, showing absolutely no concern for the people. Sure, the landholding company owns the houses, but some of the people have lived there all their lives. What are you going to do with 15 families out in weather like this with no place to go?"

He paused, staring out the window at the parking lot across the street.

"You couldn't begin to police these guys with a small army," he said.

In January, 1971, there were 7 strip-mine inspectors overseeing the work of 96 strip-mine companies at 400 different locations in the 4-county area surrounding Hazard. In all east Kentucky, there were only 32. There should have been four times that many. The inspectors are paid from $413 to $583 a month to keep a multimillion-dollar industry from destroying the mountains. Most are local men with local ties. Some once worked on strip mines themselves. Others worked as store clerks and on highway-department crews before joining the Division of Reclamation. A precious few have backgrounds in conservation work.

They are the middlemen. "We're damned if we do, damned if we don't," most of them will tell you. On one hand, they are subject to a constant harangue from strip-mine operators for being too tough in enforcing Kentucky's six-year-old strip-mining law. On the other, they're condemned for being too lenient by strip-mine critics. Harry Caudill, who first brought strip-mining to the nation's attention in 1963 with his book *Night Comes to the Cumberlands*, speaks for many. "When it comes to restraining strip-mine operators, the Division of Reclamation is as worthless as a cupful of cold spit," he says.

Bill Hayes is supervisor of strip-mine reclamation in four

counties around Hazard, one of the nation's busiest strip-mine areas. He is one of the best "enforcers," a tough, no-nonsense conservationist who was a state forester before joining the Division of Reclamation six years ago. "It was a challenge," he says. "I wanted to see if there could be a better way to strip and auger mine without causing so much damage to the land, the timber and the streams. I haven't given up yet, and I won't until we've exhausted every idea we have to control this thing."

So far neither Hayes nor anyone else has found a foolproof way to do that. They have had very little help. Until recently there had been almost no scientific inquiry into ways to make strip mining less harmful. What technical improvements have been made were developed by strip miners themselves, often under pressure from reclamation officials. "We have no textbooks to follow," Hayes says. "We're writing our own as we go along."

This type of on-the-job experimentation has severe limitations. Yet there have been advances. New methods, for example, have been devised to reduce the danger of landslides; to reseed vast stripped areas by airplane; to cut down erosion and acid runoff; to level the entire tops of mountains for use as airfields or grazing land. But only strip-mine operators can make these techniques work. All too many have shown little desire to do so. For them, genuine reclamation is a joke.

Largely it's a question of money. One U.S. Bureau of Mines environmentalist has estimated that meaningful reclamation might cost anywhere from $300 to $3,000 an acre in rugged terrain. Most operators spend just enough to get by. "You have to be constantly on the operator's back, asking him to do this and that," Hayes says. "Unless you're firm, they'll run away with you. Some of them have $3 or $4 million invested in equipment. They don't want to have that tied up doing anything but digging coal."

Even when operators obey the law, serious problems remain. The bulldozers cause many of them when they strip away the topsoil. Ideally, the topsoil should be set aside and replaced on the graded spoil banks—but strip miners consider this too troublesome, expensive and time-consuming. Thus, they are faced with trying to revegetate banks of crumbled shale and slate containing little organic matter. Even the hardiest grasses have to struggle to survive in such rubble. And when the hard rains come (up to 50 inches of rain fall on many east Kentucky slopes each year), the water cuts deep gullies, into the spoil banks and washes much of the flimsy ground cover away. One nine-year U.S. geological study of strip-mine areas in McCreary County, Kentucky, found annual erosion rates on spoil banks to range from 14.8 to 159 cubic yards per acre. The study found that the runoff literally killed all aquatic life in two adjoining streams. Six years after the strip mining was completed, almost no aquatic life had returned.

Bill Hayes has trekked across nearly every strip mine in east Kentucky. He knows the problems and offers few alibis. "We haven't found anything yet to keep that spoil from coming off the hillside because it is too unpredictable," he says. "People who continue to live in the middle of it are gambling with their lives. A flash flood could bury them under an avalanche of rock and mud."

Hayes is a native of the region, and, as is characteristic of mountaineers, views strip mining in humanistic terms. He likes to point out that most strip miners have a legal claim to the land, and that some have spent thousands of dollars in trying to reclaim it. He is suspicious of "instant experts" and outsiders who are too quick to offer solutions to Appalachian problems. He resents the greed of the strip-mine operators (one once punched him in the nose) and admits some inspectors have been "brainwashed" by strip miners' arguments and have allowed the operators to "slip out of hand." And he feels anguish at seeing mountains ravaged. "Too many houses have been destroyed, too many people have had their property damaged, too many old folks have been isolated because the strip miners have destroyed their roads," he says. "I hate to think what this country would be like if strip miners were allowed to do as they please."

He sees solutions in the same terms. "If you have boys as inspectors who are qualified and dedicated you can get the job done," he told me early one sultry June day in the height of the strip-mining season. "I've seen some good reclamation, but after a couple of years if it's obvious that it isn't working, I'll be the first to recommend an all-out ban." A week later strip-mining foes picketed Bill Hayes' office. They said the Division of Reclamation wasn't doing its job.

Dan Gibson

In the winter, the rain comes and the ground soaks it up. The temperature drops and tons of loose overburden, which strip-mine bulldozers have pushed over the hillsides, freeze. Then the mass thaws. Water seeps out. Usually it does so harmlessly. But too often the overburden moves with the water, oozing down the mountainsides like molten lava from a volcano. As it moves, roadways are blocked, homes threatened, full-grown trees snapped like toothpicks. Tons of mud slide toward creekbeds.

It was on such a day I met Dan Gibson. He is the stereotyped old mountaineer: strong and willowy at 86, thin-faced with a long arched nose and skin weathered tough by the mountain wind. He is a carpenter and he builds wooden coffins in his low-ceilinged basement workshop. They are fine, well-constructed burial boxes, stained dark mahogany on the outside, lined with white silk on the inside. He sells them to his neighbors for $150. He has spent his entire life in Knott County, Kentucky. When he was a boy, he roamed the hills hunting squirrel and possum and pulling bluegill from the clear streams. Now he pats his old squirrel rifle and says, "This is my strip-mine law. Hot lead is the only thing they understand."

Gibson lives in a pleasant cottage on a knoll above Cockles Trace Branch of Clear Creek, about six miles from the county seat of Hindman. "I came to the creek 20 years ago," he told me. "The hills were covered with game. You could kill five squirrels in an hour. Now you can't hear a quail call anywhere."

Gibson blames the change on strip mining, particularly as practiced by Bill Sturgill, long east Kentucky's biggest and most controversial strip miner. Gibson made his stand against Sturgill at about 8:30 A.M. one June day in 1965, when he began a 20-minute hike up the hollow from his place. The day before, Sturgill's bulldozers had pushed their way across Hardburly Ridge and had started tearing at a hillside owned by Gibson's stepson, Leonard Ritchie, who was stationed in Vietnam. Sturgill had a broad form deed that gave him claim to the coal under Ritchie's land. Gibson meant to put an end to it. He carried a .22-caliber rifle in one hand, a No Trespassing sign in the other.

Sturgill anticipated trouble. There had been a ruckus the night before with some of the neighbors. Shots had been fired. Now the state highway patrol was on alert.

"I slipped up on one of those big strip miners," Gibson recalled. "I was within six steps of him before he heared me. He wheeled and started to draw his gun, but I told him,

'Walk straight in front of me and get out of my way when I tell you to git.' I walked out on the point and had my boy drive the sign in the ground. I told the strip man it's a dirty shame for people to come in here and destroy the land of someone off fighting for their country overseas. Then he and that other guy retreated about 100 yards. I moved back 30 steps."

He picked a knoll to sit down on where he would have a clear shot at any bulldozer that tried to pass his No Trespassing sign. State police were called, and patrolmen, carrying shotguns, tried to persuade Gibson to leave. He refused.

At one point, his grandson, who had followed him up the hill, warned: "Looks like they're going to git you fer good. There's about 20 of them now."

Gibson replied: "Let 'em come. If I go a couple of them will go down with me."

They didn't come, but later a delegation of three lawmen approached. One dropped his .38 and stepped forward from the group. He tried to persuade Gibson to give up his post, arguing that if he wanted to stop the strip miners he should work through legal channels.

Gibson held up his rifle. "Do you see what I've got here," he said. "This is the only restraining order I need."

By late afternoon word had spread through the hollow that old Dan Gibson was holding 40 lawmen and strip miners at bay. A crowd, most of them sympathetic to his cause, gathered. Tensions mounted. At 5:00 P.M., Gibson called for the state highway patrol captain. "I told him if he'd call Bill Sturgill and get him to promise to never bother me again," he recalled, "I'll give up my gun and come back out."

Sturgill agreed and to this day his companies (he now has

sold them) have not strip mined above Clear Creek. This victory has done nothing to dampen Gibson's hatred of strip
mining. At an age when most people are ready for the geriat-
ric ward, he is a radical activist. He belongs to the
Appalachian Group to Save the Land and People, east Kentucky's most militant grassroots anti-strip-mining group.
(One of the group's most successful tactics has been to
license wide stretches of hillside as official National Rifle Association target ranges. "If they ever start stripping," one of
the group's leaders told me, "we might just decide it's time
for a little target practice.")

Gibson sees little but deceit in the claims of strip miners
and reclamation officials that strip mining can be regulated.
He cares little for scientific studies or sophisticated arguments. He cares only for the land. And as my car slipped
and skidded up the muddy roads to the top of the mountain
where the strip miners work and into the valleys around
Clear Creek, Lotts Creek and Troublesome Creek near his
home, Gibson had a story for each hillside.

"That's the Ritchie place," he said as we stopped atop one
hill. "Back in '66 one day a 'dozer came 'round the mountain
and started rolling boulders down the hill. One knocked the
porch clear off. The wife she had to grab the kids and get out
right fast."

"See that chimney. Used to be a house there," he said
three miles down the road. "A slide just pushed it away. At
the mouth of the hollow the runoff from this same strip
washed a feller's basement clear apart. He was sure it'd
wreck his place but it didn't."

"See how they tore up our roads," he added later. "Last
winter it was so bad toward Jackson that we couldn't get to
the clinic. They overload their big trucks so much they
ripped it all to pieces. A passenger car couldn't make it past.

They fixed that one, and they promised to fix some more. That's the way they work. They promise all you want then turn around and don't do it. Then they wonder what's going on when someone blows up one of their bulldozers like they did a couple weeks back."

By now we were skidding down a dirt road pockmarked with deep holes and Gibson was saying, "This water's all poison. Nothing alive in it. Too full of acid." A few days earlier the executive director of the Kentucky Coal Association had told me that acid water was not a problem in east Kentucky, and had referred me to several well-documented studies that tended to substantiate his assertion. As a result I was slightly leery of my guide—until we rounded a bend in the road. A huge clay-mud landslide covered the whole road and oozed down the mountain toward a creek. "Every time we have a little rain this happens," Gibson said as we waited for a mining company bulldozer to clear a path for us. "They couldn't hire me to sleep in any of the houses 'round here."

Thirty minutes later we were in Alice Sloan's comfortable log cabin above Cordia school. Miss Sloan is a silver-gray spinster, prim and energetic, who has spent most of her life teaching mountain children how to read and write and live in America in the twentieth century. Several times in recent months school buses from her school had narrowly escaped being pushed off the road by landslides. "I just dread the day when I'll pick up the phone and find one of our children has been buried in a strip-mine slide," she said. "We're never far away from one this time of year. Our mountains are just sliding away."

It was midafternoon when we stopped atop Hardburly Ridge. Dan Gibson pointed toward the place, a half-mile away, where he and his squirrel rifle had held the highway patrol at bay and to where a bulldozer had been blown up a few weeks before. On one side of the muddy path that passes for a road were the remnants of a once-dense forest. The other side was a barren moonscape. Notches had been cut around the mountain and the spoils hurled hundreds of feet downward into what once must have been a wooded valley. There were just the faintest hints of vegetation—a few low bushes and small clumps of grass.

Dan Gibson tugged at the brim of his brown, flat-topped felt hat. "The timber's gone, the wildlife's gone and the water's gone," he said as he looked across the barren ridge. "I've tried to save what I could, but I hate to think this is what this country is leaving my grandchildren."

13

Schools: Discrimination
in the Hills

The Rye Cove School sits in a bare spot of clay mud near the Middle Fork River in Leslie County, Kentucky. It is part of a state school system that the governor of the commonwealth has told the National Education Association "made giant strides in education in the past decade." Since anyone can remember, Rye Cove School has been where the children of War Branch, Kentucky, have gotten their first—and often last—taste of education.

The school occupies a narrow strip of bottom land about 40 yards below a gravel road that leads to Lonesome Mountain. It is a one-room frame building held above the ground by stacks of cinder blocks. Its roof is swaybacked, like a mountain mule. Once the building was painted fresh white. Today the paint has faded and there are bare spots where the white once was. Two window panes are broken on the

171

side that faces the road. Under them in the clay mud are a pile of coal and a stack of squashed milk cartons that are used to kindle the fire in the rusty potbellied stove inside. On each side of the school is an unpainted outhouse. The chalk letters on one say, "*GRILS*."

Three crude wood steps lead to the door. They are rotten and quake under even a child's weight. The teacher, Carl Wilson, was in the front of the room under a 150-watt lightbulb that dangled from the ceiling on a dusty cord. It, a similar bulb and a single string of Christmas-tree lights around a scrawny Scotch pine in the back corner were the only lights in the room.

"Always glad to have visitors," Wilson said, as if it were an everyday occurrence.

He was trying to teach the older children on the left side of the room how to divide 1,467 by 54 and 2,811 by 43. For a long time, he was silent. Then he asked if anyone had figured out the right answer. Two boys listlessly raised their hands and, in turn, gave their answers. Both were wrong. Wilson scratched more numbers on the blackboard. "Those in the sixth grade do the ones on the left; those in the eighth, the ones on the right," he said.

Tacked to the beaverboard wall above the blackboard were two pieces of faded cardboard with the words to songs printed on them in felt pen. One was an old folk ballad, "Shady Grove." The other was a Bob Dylan favorite of the mid-1960's, "Blowing in the Wind."

Wilson couldn't remember how long the Dylan song had been up front. "Multiplication tables, that's the big problem we've had here," he said. "Learning the multiplication tables. The sixth grade doesn't know them yet."

A lanky, soft-spoken mountaineer in his late fifties, Wilson wore a suede jacket over a plain flannel shirt open at the neck. He was in his fifth year at Rye Cove School and said he liked it.

"Of course, there are too many subjects," he said. "You never get around to them all. And when you do you can only spend a few minutes with each course."

Fifteen students, more or less, depending on the weather, attend Rye Cove School. They are poor—Leslie County is one of the seven poorest counties in the nation. At the start of the school year, each family fills out a registration card. This year the breadwinner in one family with children attending the school wrote "lumbering" on the blank requesting occupation. The rest said they received some type of public assistance.

The younger students sat on the right side of the room near the front so they could crowd near the rusty stove for warmth. Their features were angelic, their eyes wide and trusting.

Rye Cove's older students were on the other side of the room facing Wilson's desk and the small pile of kindling behind it. A spiny low ridge in the floor almost exactly midway between the two walls separated them from their younger brothers and sisters. Rain and heat had warped the ridge, and a crack between the two boards that formed the ridge exposed the ground below. Eight students sat on the sixth-, seventh- and eighth-grade side of the ridge. Half of them wore tattered jackets to protect them from the chill that swept through the schoolhouse walls. The stove was less than ten yards away.

The library was a single wobbly shelf against one wall. The books on it had titles like *Arithmetic in My World, Journey into America, Our Environment: Its Relation to You* and *America, Land of Freedom*. Most of the books were old and worn. One I looked at was a castoff from a rich suburban school system near Minneapolis. "Property of St. Louis Park, Minn., High School 1945," said a stamp inside its cover.

Freshly graded student papers were stacked on one shelf. On one, Billie Roark, a third grader, had written a practice sentence in almost perfectly formed longhand. "The United States Senate and House of Representatives enacts laws," it said. "The President must sign bills before they become law."

That same day Congressmen were debating a federal-aid-to-education bill, which, if passed, might someday help schools like Rye Cove. The school had already experienced congressional generosity. The free lunches and breakfasts offered students were paid for by federal funds, as was the salary of a young teaching assistant who helped Wilson. But Billie Roark's practice sentence and the debate in an august chamber in a faraway place called Washington had little relevance to what was happening in Rye Cove School on this cold November morning, or on any other morning, for that matter. Three other sentences written about a story first published in 1820 strangely had much more immediacy about them, much more to say about the day-to-day life at the school. As written in a slightly less legible hand than Billie Roark's, they were:

1. Ichabod Crane was tall and thin.
2. Ichabod taught in a one-room school.
3. The school house was made of logs.

Rye Cove School isn't typical of schools in Appalachia (although as late as 1968 there were 1,046 one- or two-room schools in the region), or even Leslie County. That it exists at all is a constant irritation to County School Superintendent Hayes Lewis.

Lewis, who started his own career in 1935 as a $48-a-month instructor in a one-room school, is painfully aware of the crippling effects schools like the one at Rye Cove have on children. Standardized tests taken throughout Leslie County have found the reading comprehension level among eighth graders in one-room schools seldom reaches much above the third-grade level.

"It makes me sick that these kids are being robbed of an education, but up till now there just hasn't been anything we could do about it," he told me after my visit to Rye Cove School. "When those kids come to high school they're lost. They stay a week or so and then we never see them again."

Leslie County reduced its number of one- and two-room schools from 72 to less than a dozen during the 1960's with the construction of 5 new, modern consolidated schools, including one named Hayes Lewis Elementary. Lewis hopes to find room to place the Rye Cove School students in one of the consolidated schools within the next year or two, thus ending Rye Cove School's history as an educational travesty. But the fact that its door was still open in the 1970-71 school year, at a time when more fortunate students in the richest nation in the world were studying laser beams and computers, shows how far education in Appalachia has to go before it catches up with the rest of the nation.

The obstacles along this path are almost endless. Some have compared them to those in the urban slums. There are similarities. Both breed distinct speech patterns, based on oral rather than written tradition, making reading and writing difficult to learn. But the problems of education in rural Appalachia are far more severe, far less receptive to change. And they command far less attention. For all practical purposes, most of the 1¼ million children of the region are invisible. They live on lonely hillsides and in half-deserted coal-camps. They are seldom seen by outsiders, or even by

businessmen in the county seats. They are given little motivation for learning. In fact, they often have to overcome
tremendous handicaps to acquire even the rudiments of an
education. And when they do so it is almost in a total
vacuum.

A typical black youth lives in a concentrated community
in a large city. His very blackness gives him a sense of iden-
tity and cohesion with the children around him. His elementary or junior high school is usually within walking distance;
at the most it is a short bus ride. He is likely to come into
daily contact with something that indicates that education is
worthwhile—an enlightened teacher, a sympathetic clergy-
man, a glance at the new Buick the factory worker down the
block just bought. Although racism may be all about him, he
may not come into a face-to-face confrontation with it until
his mid-teens, and then his community gives him a sense of
social strength that helps him endure it.

The rural Appalachian white lives in an isolated atmo-
sphere of backwardness and ignorance. He meets discrimi-
nation the day he registers for school. There is one chance in
three that his family has an income below the federal
poverty line—$3,200 for a family of four. Little has prepared
him for the world of words. He has grown up in an area with
a traditional resistance to "book learning," a place where,
until recent years, too much education was thought unnecessary—even dangerous. His environment has stressed sensitiv-
ity to people rather than to ideas. He finds it difficult to
grasp abstract concepts. School is hard for him. Little around
him indicates it's worthwhile. The results are obvious. In
1960, Appalachia contained 10 percent of the U.S. population but accounted for more than 47 percent of the nation's
functionally illiterate people.

Seldom will a rural Appalachian white come in contact

with faces and ideas foreign to his home hollow until he enters first grade—kindergartens are almost nonexistent in the region. Books and magazines often will be complete strangers to him. School may be miles from home. Often he may hike for a half-hour or more down a frozen creekbed to reach a bus stop, then sit through a long bumpy ride. By the time the day is over, he is tired and the hollow circles around his eyes show it.

Statistics speak poorly of Appalachian education once a child is in school. Almost 65 percent of those who enter first grade drop out before graduation. Those who do finish fare poorly on nationwide tests. Those who enter the Job Corps usually drop out. And almost one-third of the young men in the region fail Selective Service education tests, compared with a national failure rate of 22.8 percent.

Still, as a visitor winds his way through the region, the story of education is not in the statistics. It is in the people. It is a story of men like George Smith, 26, who stood on his rain-soaked porch in Granny's Branch, Kentucky, and said he couldn't read. "But I can sign my name *real* good."

Often it is a depressing story—perhaps a story of 30 shabbily dressed parents huddled around a potbellied stove in Teaberry, Kentucky, complaining that their children were going hungry at school because they didn't have any money to buy lunch.

Occasionally it's a story of waste, human and material—a story of hundreds of dollars worth of visual-aid equipment purchased with federal dollars sitting idle in a two-room schoolhouse because the teacher doesn't know how to use it. Or a story of an excellent vocational high school in McDowell County, West Virginia, exporting 95 percent of its graduates from the state.

Often it's a courageous story—a story of scores of teachers and administrators dedicating their lives—not infrequently under scandalous conditions and with little pay—so that some children could receive a balanced education. And of children hungry for learning. Children like Mary Ellen Noble, a crippled girl from Hot Spot, Kentucky, who trekked a mile down a slippery clay path before daybreak each day to catch a school bus, a crutch grasped in one arm, a flashlight to light the path in the other.

Above all, it is a story of not enough money and attention in the past, of a future clouded with uncertainties. In the words of Mrs. Marie Turner, former superintendent of schools in Breathitt County, Kentucky: "The children of Appalachia are as underprivileged as you'll find anywhere. Their homes are poorer, their family incomes lower, and their schools more underfinanced than anywhere I can imagine."

Education and Politics

Many school districts are hopelessly mired in politics. Often, the school superintendent is the "political boss" of the party or faction that runs the county. Even where that is not the case, the superintendent is always an important political force to reckon with. One veteran mountain teacher, now a University of Kentucky professor, explained it this way: "In most counties the school is the sole industry and largest employer. In a region where jobs are scarce, they are under tremendous political pressure to employ local people for political patronage. This forces many decisions to be made on noneducational criteria. Teachers are hired for how many votes they can deliver rather than how well they perform their jobs."

School superintendents are hired by elected school boards.
Battles for school-board seats are often the most hotly contested political races in a county. Frequently they overshad-
ow races for such locally insignificant offices as the U.S.
presidency or the governorship of the state. The stakes are
high. Superintendents control tremendous patronage machines: budgets totaling hundreds of thousands of dollars
and jobs for scores of teachers, bus drivers, lunchroom cooks,
janitors and teachers' aides. Their grip is an iron one. A teacher who opposes the political leanings of the superintendent
may suddenly find himself transferred to a school in a remote
area 30 or 40 miles from his home. Or even without a job. A
new superintendent in Pike County, Kentucky, for instance,
fired more than 200 Head Start workers after a particularly
bitter school-board contest in 1969.

Outsiders who might rock the boat are discouraged from
teaching in the region, regardless of their credentials. A
premium is put on politically safe "local folks." The result,
according to Jack Weller, author of *Yesterday's People*, is
that "too often the mountain school system becomes a closed
shop, composed of a staff of teachers who have been trained
in the same system, brought up in the same culture and
molded by the same forces as the children they attempt to
teach. Instead of challenging and stimulating children, such
a system simply perpetuates itself . . ."

In the past, dedicated educators—and there are many in
the region—have had few tools to work with. Although many
county seats and some enlightened coalcamps have schools
not markedly different from those in other parts of the nation, most schools have been grossly underfinanced and inad-
equate. In rural areas, books often have been tattered and
outdated, libraries almost nonexistent and schoolhouses di-

lapidated. For years teachers with emergency certificates working in one-, two- or three-room schoolhouses were the rule rather than the exception.

Local finances have been meager. And with the only natural resources of the region—its coal, natural gas and lumber—rapidly being depleted, there is little hope for increased local support in the future. The region opted out on its hope of the past—taxing coal—and now there are no reserves. "We really don't have the money to pay for decent education," Alex Eversole, superintendent of schools in Perry County, Kentucky, has said. "Our only hope was drained away years ago by the coal interests and our failure to tax them. Why, I can remember just in my lifetime Perry County could have anything it wanted in education with just a minimal tax. But the money all went to New York and Pittsburgh. We were left without any."

In recent years, increased state aid—most often the result of increased sales taxes—has improved teachers' salaries and enabled local districts to undertake modest building projects. Today modern new schools dot most Appalachian counties. The use of emergency-certified teachers is rapidly disappearing. And one-room schoolhouses, like the one at Rye Cove, are becoming a thing of the past.

Money, however, remains in short supply. Scores of dilapidated school buildings still scar the landscape. Many school districts spend half their resources transporting students to and from school over treacherous winding roads. Teaching supplies are often limited. Salaries continue to fall well below the national average. A beginning teacher in Leslie County, Kentucky, for instance, earns only $5,358 his first year. The same job pays $7,183 in Seattle, Washington. Turnover is high—14.2 percent per year compared to a national average of 8.2 percent. Many teachers are old. Young teachers are needed, yet of those hired, 65 percent leave by the end of their first four years, usually for higher-paying jobs in other states.

Many schools are too small. Preschool education is almost nonexistent; in 1967, for instance, an Appalachian Regional Commission survey reported that less than 2 percent of the region's school districts had any type of kindergarten. Vocational education is just beginning to spread. But according to another study by the same commission, it often offers outdated programs of little practical use. And most often it ignores training for the region's only viable industry—coal mining.

The massive federal education programs of the last decade, most of them originating from the Elementary and Secondary Education Act of 1964, kept the schools from sinking even further into futility. Hundreds of thousands of federal dollars flowed into almost every school district. Slide projectors, phonographs, libraries, remedial-reading teachers and physical-education instructors made their first appearances in hundreds of schools. Hot-lunch programs, many providing a free breakfast and midday meal to poor children, blossomed. Teachers' aides were placed in many classrooms. New vocational schools sprang up. Head Start classes were offered to thousands of preschool youngsters. And their older brothers and sisters found after-school jobs in the Neighborhood Youth Corps.

All such changes were welcomed. But often the programs were not directed at the region's greatest needs. As a result, their impact has been largely hit-and-miss. One problem from the outset was that, unlike the case of the urban ghetto student, there was little to guide policymakers toward meeting the needs of rural Appalachian youth. Too often it was assumed that the problems were the same wherever deprived children lived. Appalachian educators had little success in persuading Washington bureaucrats otherwise. "We've never been able to get it into their heads that we aren't a bunch of dirty-eared, uncouth hillbillies, who don't know what we're doing," one superintendent told me.

In some cases, federal programs clearly discriminated against small Appalachian school districts. A few required local matching funds, an almost impossible commodity to come by in most school districts. Others didn't provide adequate transportation allowances. Many had restrictions against spending federal funds for new buildings, which Appalachian educators generally consider to be their biggest need. And almost all had strings attached and began on a crash basis.

Another problem has been a lack of trained personnel. How can a school start a cultural-enrichment program, for example, if it can't even find a qualified art or music teacher to hire? In an even more crucial lack, few school districts in the mid-1960's could call on anyone trained in grantmanship —the all-important art of finding and wooing federal and foundation grants. "I know there is a lot of money out there that we qualify for, but don't know about," said one east Kentucky superintendent from a county where 77 percent of the children are classified as economically deprived. "City schools with bigger, better-trained staffs know what's out there. And they keep better records. They can just reach up and get their data off the shelf. We have to search and scratch for ours. They're funded before we even hear about any new programs."

Few Appalachian educators can document how they've been discriminated against by the federal aid-to-education programs of the 1960's. None would advise that the programs be disbanded. Most would, however, ask that they be expanded to take into account the special problems of finance and isolation of the region.

Among the educators, Title I of the Elementary and Secondary Education Act of 1964 is the largest and most popular—if for no other reason than that it offers the most money. Alloting more than half a million dollars a year to some county school districts, it has set up remedial reading programs, bought much needed audio-visual equipment, paid salaries for school nurses and social workers and in some cases gotten pet building programs off the ground. Title II of the same act has financed the first libraries in dozens of schools. Title IV has built new vocational schools throughout the region. Among other programs common to most Appalachian school districts are the Neighborhood Youth Corps, Title III—the experimental end of the 1964 education act—Teachers Corps, and, of course, Head Start. Head Start runs a weak second in popularity to Title I, largely because until recently it was controlled in most counties by antipoverty groups rather than by school systems. Moreover, in a region rampant with poverty, a surprisingly small percentage of children are enrolled in Head Start classes. According to one study by the Appalachian Regional Commission, less than 10 percent of the 600,000 four- and five-year-olds in the region were enrolled.

Appalachian educators are not without fault in regard to federal money. Few, for instance, have used it to bring new ideas into the classroom or to develop innovative programs. And in some cases, local administrators and state education officials have actually sabotaged programs designed to aid their schools and the region's poor, either by neglect, lack of interest or calculated design. The national school-lunch program offers an example. Since the program's founding in 1946, Congress has stressed over and over the national ideal that no child should be deprived of a school lunch for lack of money, and it has committed billions of dollars and mountains of surplus commodities to that end. In April, 1968, however, a national group of churchwomen called the Committee on School Lunch Preparation reported that children with the greatest need for free lunch were the least likely to get it and pointed to weak local support and the lack of firm federal guidelines for determining need as the chief reasons.

Responding to this criticism, the U.S. Department of Agriculture issued, in October, 1968, a detailed list of regulations on how free and reduced-price lunch moneys should be used. The department's policy was clear enough. In short, it said all needy children should be given free or reduced-price lunches. But more than a year later these instructions were being largely ignored or circumvented in dozens of Kentucky counties. In some, a family had to be nearly destitute before its children could qualify for free lunches. In others, there were wide inequities in who the local school district considered "needy." A mother of five whose only income was a $185 monthly check from Aid to Families with Dependent Children had to pay 25 cents to buy each of her two children lunch if she lived in Perry County, Kentucky, for example. If she moved to Lexington, the nearest large city, her children would eat free. If she moved to nearby Lee County, she'd pay 10 cents a meal. Some counties left the matter up to the whim of the teacher or local principal. The lunch guidelines in Owsley County, Kentucky, noted that a "self employed farmer" who "grows his own hogs" and "has a wife who sews may have an income of just under $1,200" and be able to pay for lunches for "1 or 2 children." But, it added, a "family with two school age children and a mother who is a welfare recipient may not."

The results of the inequities were predictable. Thousands of children were deprived of the free lunches that Congress had intended them to receive. In mid-1968, the state Department of Education reshuffled the federal moneys it had received to provide lunches for 60,000 poor children. The Division of School Lunch, a spokesman said, had no other choice because local school officials could find only 20,000 needy youngsters to eat them. An even more damning indictment was found in a report sponsored by the Children's Foundation, of Washington, D.C. It revealed that Kentucky had "diverted" $900,000 intended for school lunches for the poor to other purposes. The money was used, said the report, to "hold down the prices of regular school lunches, in effect benefiting middle-class youngsters and diluting a special effort to provide an adequate diet for the poor."

Jackson County, Kentucky, in the Appalachian foothills, was only one of the places the lunches surfaced as a bitterly contested issue. In 1968, a school-lunch committee, made up almost entirely of poor people, found that only 35 percent of the underprivileged schoolchildren in the county who qualified for free lunches actually received them, and that scores of families didn't even know the lunches were available. In addition, many children were required to work for lunches, and often children sat, hungry, in the same lunchrooms where more fortunate classmates were eating. For months the committee held meetings with poverty workers, wrote letters to the Department of Agriculture and gathered signatures on petitions. Eventually, it pressured School Superintendent Otis Johnson into issuing the county's first public guidelines on who was eligible to receive free lunches. The committee was still dissatisfied. It maintained that the guidelines were too high (under them a family of six with two children in school could have an income as low as $2,652 and still have to pay full lunch prices) and that dozens of youngsters were staying home from school because they didn't have enough money to buy lunch.

I asked Johnson about this in a visit to his office on the outskirts of McKee, Kentucky. He refused to discuss the matter, except to say that most of the county's poor were receiving free or reduced-price lunches.

Less that ten miles away, near Sand Gap, Kentucky, Mrs. Reba Phillips had a forlorn look on her young face. It was Thursday, but her three children weren't in school, and they hadn't been in two of the past three days. Her children's application for free school lunches had been rejected because her husband's income was too high—about $3,100 a year, well below the U.S. Office of Economic Opportunity's poverty guidelines—she said.

"Sure I'm worried about them not being in school," Mrs. Phillips told me as the children—a first, a third and a fourth grader—played in the living room. "They get behind in their work and it's hard to catch up.

"But what can I do," she continued. "I don't have any money for them to buy lunch with. And I don't have anything to send with them."

14

The Poverty Warriors

Tom Fletcher was waiting on the porch of the house he paid $100 for when the President of the United States came to call. They sat on a pile of lumber, Fletcher and Lyndon Baines Johnson.

"He was a common-talkin' man," Fletcher, a lifelong Republican, remembers. "He asked how I was doing. I told him there weren't much work around here. And there sure weren't."

Fletcher, a soft-spoken sawmill worker, had earned only $400 the previous year, mostly from odd jobs. That didn't go far with a family of eight children, he told Johnson.

The President nodded in agreement. He had once been poor himself. "He said he would try to get some help, to get us some jobs maybe," Fletcher recalls.

He paused. "Then I said any man who don't have a job is

poor—I could sure have used a job. Lot of other folks 'round here told him the same thing."

The president and Fletcher sat on the pile of 2-by-4's for 20 more minutes. They chatted about life on Rockcastle Creek, where the Fletchers live, and conditions in Martin County, Kentucky, then the fourth-poorest county in the nation.

Finally, Johnson rose to leave. "Now you remember what I said, keep those children in school. I mean the girls, too, as well as the boys," he said.

Fletcher, then 38, and his wife Nora nodded with approval as Secret Service agents whisked Johnson away down KY 3 toward Inez, the Martin County seat. Fletcher had a third-grade education. His wife had finished sixth grade. "It's hit me hard . . . not being schooled," he said.

The President had impressed both of them. They were sure his visit "would bring us some luck." Their story would become that of the Appalachian War on Poverty in miniature.

Later that evening Johnson, back in Washington, gathered the governors of seven Appalachian states at the White House. He told them that he was deeply moved by what he had seen that day and that he planned to ask Congress for a massive redevelopment program "to set the people of this region out on the bright highway of hope." The governors were elated. Four years of debate and deprivation had passed since Kennedy first discovered poverty in the hills of southern West Virginia. Kennedy had promised help, but he was killed before he could deliver it. Now Johnson renewed the pledge. New highways, development loans, job-training programs and welfare services were promised.

That was April 24. By August 20, when Johnson signed the Economic Opportunity Act of 1964, its scope had grown. It was now a national effort far bolder than the one he had told the governors about a few months before and far more controversial than the job-training and food-distribution programs Kennedy had advocated during the spring of 1960.

The new programs called not just for economic development but for a social reformation. As a matter of political expediency, the Appalachia effort would be split in two parts. Human-development—people—programs would start immediately and would become the responsibility of the Office of Economic Opportunity (OEO), the new national antipoverty agency. Because Johnson feared Congress wouldn't buy a special poverty effort for Appalachia, economic-development programs for the region would have to wait a year. They would eventually come under the auspices of the Appalachian Regional Commission (ARC), which the region's governors had formed in 1960.

Within months, millions of federal dollars descended on the mountain valleys with all the gusto of a well-intentioned avalanche. A new generation of federally supported agencies with alphabet-soup names—OEO, ARC, VISTA (Volunteers in Service to America), NYC (Neighborhood Youth Corps), CAA's (Community Action Agencies), to name just a few—invaded every county seat. Surveys were commissioned, committees and commissions established, programs launched. Unemployed old men—"Happy Pappies"—were put to work sweeping streets and clearing brush from roadsides. Children were given jobs after school. Sewing classes sprang up for mothers. Ivy League professors, college dropouts, schoolteachers, hucksters, missionaries and ex-civil-rights workers jockeyed to get part of the action.

The mountains had never seen anything quite like it. "This conglomeration came on us like a mass of jelly the size of Mt. Everest," wrote Kentucky humorist Alan Trout. "It has swept over towns, people, rivers, knobs, and institutions. Everything in its path has been covered with jelly."

Tom Fletcher did well by the jelly. A year after the President came to call, the Great Society was making him into an auto mechanic in a Manpower Development and Training class in Inez, five miles down the road from his home. The classes paid him $42 a week, or roughly four times what he earned the previous year. This was enough for him to buy a $143 cookstove and a $115 bedroom suite for his four-room house. He also put electricity in his house for the first time and bought a set of new teeth for himself and another for his wife.

"They cost $118 for each of us," Mrs. Fletcher, a hospitable, painfully thin woman, told a visitor. "It does look like we've done some better."

Those were heady days, both in Rockcastle Creek and in Washington. The war in Appalachia and the nation's ghettos was still more important than the one in Vietnam. Pollsters found that a majority of Americans supported its goals, if not always its methods. Congress sensed this sympathy and some of the boldest legislation since the New Deal moved through its chambers with astonishing ease. By the end of the War on Poverty's first year in operation, director Sargent Shriver boasted that one or more of its programs was operating in 2,742 of the nation's counties, including all but 4 of the 182 poorest. More than half a million children had been rushed through hastily assembled Head Start classes. In all, the War on Poverty had "reached" one-sixth of the nation's 34 million poor in just 12 months, he said. The message was soothing. Johnson added to the euphoria. "Dole is dead," he declared with the signing of the Appalachian Regional Act of 1965.

Dole, of course, was not dead, or even in ill health. In fact, it could be argued that some of the new poverty programs deepened the "culture of dependency." Eastern Kentucky's "Happy Pappy" program was a good example. Since it was designed to put money in the pockets of unemployed fathers, antipoverty officials insisted on calling it a "training" program and enrolling its participants into a few hours of classes each week. Actually it was a good "income-maintenance" program and put bread on the tables of many hungry families. The training classes were little more than a charade, however. "All they learned was how to eat regularly," one official quipped when the program was phased out.

But these were things easily overlooked. Bulldozers were cutting new roads through the mountains. Almost every week there was an announcement that this or that agency in almost every county had received some sort of new grant for $50,000 or $100,000.

These were the hopeful days before Vietnam had become a national tragedy, the days before the generation gap, pot or urban riots. People wanted to believe that government made a difference. They wanted to believe that Congress could pass a law and racism would end, that poverty would be eliminated. Viewpoints became distorted. When the morning fog lifted from the Cumberland Mountains, almost every "objective" newsman who visited eastern Kentucky could see some signs of prosperity in the next valley.

It mattered not that there was little concrete evidence to substantiate the "feeling," or that it was obvious that the poverty programs were "reaching" only a handful of the region's poor. There was simply so much movement that *something* must be happening. Mountain boys were being packed off to Job Corps centers; their little sisters were in Head Start classes close to home; their mothers were sewing patchwork quilts to sell at $15 each; their fathers were repairing bridges and building roadside parks with the Happy Pappies. Food stamps were stretching food budgets and improving diets.

College students—500 in the Appalachian Volunteer program in 1966 alone—flocked to the hills to save the poor and hope that they would be redeemed in the process. One-room schoolhouses were repaired and painted for the first time in a generation. New sewer and water projects were planned. Dozens of poor were hired to search out the indigent, Head Start aides and antipoverty field workers. Teachers said the new money showed up in the clothes kids wore to school. Businessmen said it showed up in their cash registers and in the offices thrown up to house the new bureaucrats. In Jackson, Kentucky, banker Phil Smith told a *Washington Post* reporter that bank deposits had doubled in his county since 1960 and that it was impossible to get inside his bank on the first of the month.

Where did the money come from?

"From these government programs, of course," he said. "It's like living in a socialist state. Since Medicare started, the drugstores can hardly fill the orders. The doctors are so busy it's hard to get an appointment. The grocery stores are cashing in on the food stamps. My own business is the same way. From 85 to 90 percent of the checks we clear are government checks. I don't like it but we've gone too far to turn back."

And there were the meetings. Every self-respecting civic leader had two or three a week at which he would gather with his contemporaries to plan how tourist industry could be lured to the mountains and to gripe about how the poverty programs were wasting money and making it impossible for them to hire anyone at a decent wage—$1 an hour.

The poor were meeting also. Young antipoverty workers

scoured hillsides and hollows to bring the poor and bedraggled together. The poor talked about how to take over the spending of their poverty money—"our money"—from the "courthouse gangs," or how to make welfare departments and school boards more responsive to the needs of the poor, or how to stop strip miners, or how to get better roads for their hollows.

Many of the antipoverty workers were from outside the region. The mountaineer first greeted them with curiosity. Naturally distrustful of strangers, he wondered why he was attracting so much attention. Some of the workers wore beards; others, short skirts. The mountaineer wondered about their dress and manner. Most were well educated. A few were from wealthy, well-known families. One tiny West Virginia village found Jay Rockefeller, son of the president of Chase Manhattan Bank, in its midst. Appalachian Volunteers counted a daughter of former Kentucky Governor Bert Combs among their number. The mountaineer wondered what "these folks" were up to. But gradually he accepted many of them as part of the new Appalachian scene, and some hollows moved toward the OEO ideal of "maximum feasible participation."

By 1967 these "community action groups" had grown in strength to the point at which the most optimistic of their young organizers said the poor were "ready to rise up in every county of Kentucky." Although the groups were generally ineffectual, some had scored notable victories. In Mingo County, West Virginia, for example, one group led an impressive onslaught on corrupt voting practices that had paralyzed the county for decades. Another organization, called the Appalachian Group to Save the Land and the People, stopped strip miners from ruining the hillsides above the homes of farmers in Knott and Pike counties, Kentucky.

The region's middle class suddenly found itself on the defensive. Most resented any hint that their region was any poorer than anyplace else. Many had registered resistance to the War on Poverty since its inception. "We don't want to be pitied, or done onto," one Letcher County, Kentucky, principal lectured me in the spring of 1968. "We just want to be left alone."

Politicians found themselves particularly vulnerable. "Peaceful citizens all at once are spouting hate," said one Kentucky legislator. "The organizers are teaching class hatred. The business people are 'big shots.' The county officials are 'power-structure bosses.' Let a man find a job making $800 a month and he becomes an 'enemy.' "

The Demise

It is hard to pinpoint just where, but somewhere along the line many of the principles and assumptions the War on Poverty operated on began to catch up with it. For many, these assumptions suddenly became myths.

Myth One: The nation would support a long-term commitment to end poverty. In theory, the early days of the poverty effort were to be a period of experimentation. Community Action Agencies were to be formed in every county to design programs to fit their individual needs. OEO would finance the best ones, modestly at first but increasingly each year as they proved their worth.

This theory was based on the assumption that OEO's funds would increase dramatically each year. Early estimates were that OEO would have $6 billion to spend by 1969. The Vietnam War wrecked all hope for this. By 1969 OEO's budget totaled only $2 billion, just a half billion more than in 1966. The results were obvious. Too little was expected to go too far. "Everywhere the commitment was too small," said Whitesburg, Kentucky, attorney-author Harry Caudill. "It was like pouring mercurochrome on a cancer."

Myth Two: The nation had the moral stamina to support a long-term commitment to ending poverty. As one veteran of five years of the War on Poverty put it, "Liberals [he considered himself one] are always coming out with this or that grandiose scheme to save someone. They convince the policymakers of their great wisdom, then jump in and for a few years make it their great cause. Their hearts bleed and they question everyone else's motives. But they always fink out and jump on the next bandwagon whether it be civil rights, poverty, hunger or ecology. I've seen it happen too many times."

Myth Three: Poverty can be cured with something other than money. There are many symptoms of poverty—poor education, malnutrition, isolation, broken homes, etc.—but the only universal characteristic of all poor people is that they don't have enough money. The easiest—and most expensive—way to correct this would be to give the poor people more money. But this wasn't OEO's bag. Instead it based the War on Poverty on the self-help principle that the poor could help themselves overcome poverty by organizing together. This struck at important spiritual aspects of poverty—lack of aspiration, loneliness and powerlessness—but when poor people found that all they would get out of the War on Poverty were moral victories, and that all the money would go to the administrators, they deserted it in droves.

Myth Four: The poor could organize their way out of poverty—"maximum feasible participation," the OEO called it. Actually, this is more half-truth than myth. Community organizations are valuable pressure groups, but the only effective groups I've seen have three important elements—strong leadership, a coherent issue and attainable goals. This combination is rare, particularly among poor people who by definition are those least able to take care of themselves.

Appalachia—where many of the poor are too old, too infirm, too young or too defeated to join any groups—presents special problems. For one thing, its geography and isolation make it extremely difficult even to gather a group. For another, sociologists, missionaries and educators have traditionally found mountaineers unwilling to give up their independence to work with organized groups. "Many of the organizers weren't really interested in the mountains," one young college-educated North Carolinian told me. "They just had their own cause that they wanted to pawn off on the mountain people. And if there is one thing that mountain people don't like, it is to be used by fair-weather warriors or hucksters."

Myth Five: Politics could be kept out of poverty. The War on Poverty's founding fathers distrusted local political units —they hadn't been responsive in the past and they weren't likely to change unless forced to do so. Thus, a decision was made to administer poverty programs free of city-hall or county-courthouse control—primarily through newly formed "Community Action Agencies."

This approach sounded good on paper and had the added appeal of giving a bipartisan air to the new war. But it didn't work—at least not in most parts of Appalachia. Perhaps it was foolish even to dream it could. As one political appointee to a $10,000-a-year poverty job told me, "We've got an unbelievable amount of politics in our schools and churches. It's pretty naive to think we wouldn't have it in our poverty programs."

Poverty programs posed a real threat to mountain politicians. They provided the poor, as well as opposing political factions, with a power base and placed a tremendous amount of patronage at their disposal. If effectively organized, the new groups could be used as vehicles to throw old-liners out. Some shrewd political pros sized up the situation immediately and moved to gain control of the CAA boards and staff members. Others waited until groups of poor people began demanding better schools and better roads, then screamed that OEO was financing the overthrow of local governments. The local politicians found many sympathetic ears in Washington.

Myth Six: The federal government could marshal a unified effort to help the poor. It couldn't. Within months after the Great Society crash programs began, they became entangled in an incredible web of confusion, red tape and cross purposes. One group of Kentucky counties, for example, found that each of three separate agencies—OEO, ARC and the Department of Agriculture—was throwing up its own housing program. Dozens of other counties discovered they had to set up separate "grass-roots" links to five different agencies —OEO, ARC, EDA (the Economic Development Administration, HUD (the Department of Housing and Urban Development) and HEW (the Department of Health, Education and Welfare)—to qualify for programs. Each agency had its own meetings, its own staff, its own surveys and its own pet projects. Each thought its plan to save Appalachia was best. No one wanted to talk to anyone else about it.

Consider the OEO and the ARC. Both were created for the same purpose—to help a deprived region. And both spent millions in the same remote counties. Yet even today they hardly speak to one another. Their differences are philosophical. The ARC is a bricks-and-mortar agency not too interested in people. It believes that Appalachia will never develop economically until it can offer prospective industry the same kinds of roads, schools, hospitals and services that the rest of the nation already possesses. OEO is a "people" agency. Its programs are based on the idea that the mountain poor need "human development" before they can throw off their bonds of hopelessness and welfarism and be ready to take the jobs the ARC would bring to their doorstep. Even given the supposition that both approaches might have merit, there is no excuse for their not being coordinated. But "coordination" is a dirty word among bureaucrats, even well-meaning ones. To this day each agency goes about its work with nothing but contempt for the other.

The Scene Today

The myths and realities have taken their toll. Battle fatigue has set in on the War on Poverty in Appalachia. The drama, the idealism and the hope that characterized it in its early stages have faded away.

Visiting antipoverty projects in eastern Kentucky and West Virginia, one finds the old excitement and fervor dissipated. Many of the antipoverty administrators are more interested in defending their programs and jobs than in helping the poor. They are careful in their conversations, conservative in their approaches. Their programs have shifted toward creating jobs, not social revolutions. They are increasingly beholden to local political powers. Some have become mere extensions of entrenched political machines.

The poverty program has long been in trouble with Congress and the Nixon administration in Washington. Those on the front lines in Appalachia know it. "This agency will self-destruct—soon," says a sign tacked on the wall of one West Virginia poverty agency. Only clever political maneuvering by east Kentucky Congressman Carl Perkins, chairman of the powerful House Education and Labor Committee, saved the OEO from destruction in 1970 when it last came up for renewal. Many poverty workers are skeptical that he can pull off such a coup again.

The introspective among them are asking themselves the obvious: What will be left when we're gone? What lasting impact will the War on Poverty have had on the region? Discounting several notable exceptions, the answer almost always is, "Very little."

"I'm afraid we blew it," says Loyal Jones, former executive director of the Council of Southern Mountains, the region's oldest antipoverty organization. "The Sixties were our golden opportunity. Now, I don't know if we'll get another chance."

That's not to say the federal billions haven't been noticed. Coupled with a coal boom, they've brought a new prosperity to most county-seat towns. Most now claim new government buildings, health centers and vocational schools. The region's middle-class is bigger and more prosperous than ever before. It's now not unusual to find a $35,000 home with a new speedboat in the driveway within shouting distance of a shanty that rents for $15 a month. Modern supermarkets and discount stores have sprung up in all but the most backwoods counties. Some inhabitants have found a "social conscience" extremely rewarding. A new doctor coming into many areas now can count on clearing $30,000 or more his first year in practice, thanks to federal medical programs for the poor and the aged. One established Campton, Kentucky, physician, in fact, collected $106,122 in Medicaid payments in 1969—and still complained he was underpaid.

It's now easier to get into and out of Appalachia than ever before. New roads financed by the ARC have cut through mountains to open up remote areas to tourism and future industrial development. Jobs are more plentiful. The commission claims that 350,000 new jobs have been generated in the region since 1965. But even in these two instances, there is a gap between promise and performance, and between the two faces of Appalachia.

Most new jobs, for example, are in the far northern and far southern reaches of the region, not normally thought of as being part of Appalachia by anyone but the commission. As a matter of policy, the ARC has favored these areas with development investments on the grounds that they have a better "growth potential" than more remote areas. From 1965 to 1969, for instance, the commission allocated more than $38.5 million for industrial development to such areas as Pittsburgh, Elmira, New York, and Erie, Pennsylvania. At the same time, hard-core poverty areas of eastern Kentucky received only $5.2 million.

Nor have the roads reached many of the hard-core Appalachian poor. Although the commission had approved construction of 2,604 miles of roadway by mid-1970, only 308 miles had actually been completed. West Virginia, the state with the most severe transportation crisis in the region, for all practical purposes didn't even get started on a road-building program until 1968, three years after the commission was formed. At this writing, West Virginia has been allotted funds for 410 miles of highway, more than any other two states combined. Yet only 43 miles have been completed, largely due to incompetence in the state highway department. In addition, many critics have condemned the new highways already in use as outmoded because many are of the three-lane variety, long considered obsolete in other parts of the country.

The ARC discounts these setbacks as part of the slow process of economic and social change, and points to the great popularity of its programs among Congressmen and Chamber of Commerce groups. "You won't find what has happened in central Appalachia out there," John D. Whisman, until recently states' regional representative to the commission and thus its number-two man, told me in an interview. "What has changed is government policy . . . we've concentrated on a program design that will deliver what the people need. In 10 or 20 years we'll see the results. Perhaps as early as the late 1970's we'll see an in-migration because we'll have the jobs, the educational facilities and the services waiting."

In the meantime, the overwhelming fact of life in Appalachia is that the poor are still there, most with the same basic problems they had a decade ago. Per capita income in eastern Kentucky, for instance, is still roughly half the national average. The unemployment rate, although lower than before, is still cruelly high. In 1969, 11 percent of the work force in eastern Kentucky and 8.4 percent of that in West Virginia was unemployed, compared with a national average of 3.5 percent. And this doesn't take into account the thousands of men who have simply given up looking for jobs and whose names aren't included in the statistics. On two occasions I've interviewed more than a dozen seemingly able-bodied men in a single day who claimed that they had literally no income for months at a time and that their families would starve if they couldn't borrow a few dollars to purchase federal food stamps.

The out-migration continues unabated in the hard-core areas of central Appalachia. Eastern Kentucky showed a population loss of 64,114 in the 1960's; West Virginia 162,710, or roughly 17,000 more than it experienced between 1950 and 1960.

If the poor have changed, it's only in that they have become more cynical and more distrustful of schemes to save them. "It's like this," Willie Johnson, who operates a small fruit stand outside Manchester, Kentucky, told me. "The programs have been okay, but those that really needs them don't get the help—and those that don't, they figure out a way to get a piece of the action."

A disabled coal miner in Mingo County, West Virginia, put it even more cynically. "It was just something to keep some of the people quiet while the politicians took the rest of them to the cleaners. It was like they threw a scrap of meat in the center and made everyone into wild dogs trying to get a bite of it. The bigshots ended up with all the big, juicy chunks. The poor people got the scraps."

The victories for the poor *are* hard to measure.

There was a bridge built across a creek near Hindman, Kentucky . . . the school clothes a father in Logan County, West Virginia, bought for his second-grade daughter with money he earned on a job-training program . . . a strong fight against strip mining in Pike County, Kentucky . . . a job for a mother in a gourmet restaurant run by the poor in Williamson, West Virginia . . . a 55-year-old grandfather who learned arithmetic in a training class ("Any man should go to school till he can figure," he told me. "I didn't know nothing about 'rithmetic. Now I can figure with anybody.") . . . a high-school junior in Keystone, West Virginia, who didn't drop out of school because of the $1.25 an hour she earned after school in the Neighborhood Youth Corps.

Tragically, the defeats are better known.

Tom Fletcher, the "typical poor man" that Lyndon Johnson visited in 1964, is one of them. I stopped by his place one November day. It was cold. Rain had fallen for three days, and now it had turned to sleet. Fletcher was watching it from the worn couch in his living room. His handshake was weak. He said he hadn't worked regularly in more than two years, ever since he broke his right leg in four

places when a tile fell on it as he was doing road work for the
state.

"There's a whole lot of work around, but there's not much
for me," he said. "Seems everyone is looking for the younger
fellers, the teen-agers and such."

The training program in which he had taken part in the
year after the President's visit hadn't helped. "Never learned
nothing in that," he said. "Never had nothing to work on.
Mostly we sat around. Oh, once in a while someone would
bring a car in and maybe we'd put in a new ball joint or a
couple plugs. Never amounted to much, though."

The family still doesn't own a car, or anything beyond the
meager furnishings of the house Nora Fletcher keeps as spot-
less as an operating room. The Fletchers live hand-to-mouth.
Each month the local antipoverty agency gives the family a
few dollars to help buy food stamps. Otherwise, Fletcher
said, the family lives off "the little bit I draw for my daughter," who apparently receives public assistance for her two
children, and whatever odd jobs he can pick up. He has
looked for steady work, but without success.

"Don't seem much hope for a man my age," Fletcher said.
He was 43.

15

The Courthouse Gang

It was the dullest election day anyone could remember. No one was shot; free whiskey was scarce; vote buying, though not absent, was at an apparent minimum. Everywhere you went, people said, "You should have been here two years ago, or even last spring." Warren A. Cline, who died on January 13, 1961, but continued voting for the next three elections, wasn't voting. Neither was A. D. Carters, whose death in 1956 didn't stop his vote from being counted in almost every election for a decade. Nor was Carlos Dowden, who has lived across the Tug River over in Kentucky since anyone can remember. Nor was Wendell Davis, who moved to Ohio years ago.

At Precinct No. 3 on Vincent Street in Williamson Hollow, West Virginia, the turnout was light. "I heared they ain't givin' nothing for a vote," explained an elderly man in a

Navy pea coat. "Ever hear such? Why do they suspect a man to vote if he don't get nothing?" Inside the Precinct No. 3 polling place at the Mingo County Curriculum Center, which used to be the old Liberty, or "colored," high school, the stench of cheap whiskey was heavy. Jack Owens was nervous.

"Don't know what that smell is," he said. "Quiet election, very quiet."

"Vote buying? I've heard of it, but never 'round here. Up in Logan or Campbell county maybe, but never here."

Williamson Hollow and Precinct No. 3 are mostly black. Jack Owens is white, but that doesn't matter because he is held in high repute in Mingo County, West Virginia—such high repute that when a Republican became governor, Jack Owens, a Democrat, got a job as maintenance supervisor at the Mingo County courthouse. Maintenance supervisor was a good job because while 13 former state road and liquor-sales workers were assigned to do maintenance work at the same courthouse, there really was only enough work for 2 or 3. Jobs aren't really that important, anyway. Mostly they're something to be paid for doing between elections. Elections are what Jack Owens is good at. That's why he was top election official at Precinct No. 3.

The reason Owens was so nervous this election day is that he is a machine man and the machine had fallen on bad days. For almost two years the FBI, the Department of Justice and a series of federal grand juries had been probing reports of election irregularities in Mingo County. Some of the investigators thought dead people shouldn't vote and live people shouldn't be paid for voting. These odd ideas had obvious political consequences, some of which were already being felt by the machine. In the 1970 spring primary, for example, an insurgent upset machine boss Noel Floyd in a race for the state Senate seat Floyd had held for eight years. Three months later, a federal grand jury indicted Floyd and another county official on charges of conspiring to spend $50,000 buying votes in the 1968 general election, charges of which both later were acquitted.

Owens blamed all this on West Virginia Secretary of State Jay Rockefeller, who had joined with poverty workers and local reform elements to press for election reform in Mingo County. As Owens described it, Rockefeller was an outsider, a young whippersnapper with questionable ideals and motives who was out to "buy this state" so he could become governor like his two uncles—New York Governor Nelson Rockefeller and former Arkansas Governor Winthrop Rockefeller.

"He's out to ruin all the good people of West Virginia," Owens said. His shiny purple silk suit shook with anger as he spoke.

"Noah Floyd is the finest man who ever lived in this county. He has done more for this place than any man in history. He's just a good, God-fearing gentleman."

Small-town Bosses

One of the great tragedies of American political science is that its literature abounds with tales of big-city bosses and their machines but seldom mentions anything about the small-town bosses who run their counties with as much chicanery as ever imagined by a tabloid editor. A Daley in Chicago, a Pendergast in Kansas City, a Curley in Boston can rise to national prominence for his election-day antics, but an equally sincere power broker in downstate Illinois or the hills of Appalachia will seldom gain any notoriety outside of his county seat.

Eastern Kentucky and southern West Virginia are particu-

larly rife with boss rule. Here politics isn't just a civic exercise in which the citizenry goes to the polls every year or so,
it is a full-time occupation, a way of life, played with the
same blind devotion that a tenement dweller in Harlem
gives to the numbers racket or a bettor at Hialeah brings to
the racetrack. Part of the reason for this phenomenon lies in
the isolation of the region, and the lack of alternative activities. "Living here," one mountaineer explained, "there's only
three things to do—fight, chase women or get into politics."

Many smart ones get into politics. The choice is logical
and often necessary, particularly in the smallest and most
remote counties. In many of them, most of the decent jobs in
the county depend on political connections. If a man wants
to work in the county schools or county courthouse or the
state highway department or the local antipoverty agency,
either he or someone in his family ought best have some political ties. Once on the job, the worker-politician must play
it safe. Boat-rocking is seldom tolerated. Loyalty and service
are, especially on election day and when the office bagman
comes around selling tickets for the local party's annual
fund-raising dinner.

If the worker-politician is young and aspires to higher
things, he must wait, doing what is expected of him, little
more, little less. Eventually, if someone dies or a factional
battle splits the local party, the young loyalist can make a
bid for elective public office. The most skillful and ambitious
among them seek out the prestigious offices of county judge,
county magistrate or commissioner, county clerk, county tax
assessor, circuit court judge, sheriff, state representative or
state senator, or the appointive but politically potent job of
school superintendent.

Issues are seldom important in these races. This bothers no
one. While other men look for ways to preserve their envi-

ronment or travel to the moon, mountain voters dote on a diet of kinship loyalties, promises of good roads and tales of patriotic exploits in wars long past. It would be a mistake, however, to think this state of affairs makes for dull elections. Appalachian campaigns are among the nation's most bitter and hard fought. Candidates and their supporters plot their strategy for months. There is money to be collected from patronage workers, election commissioners to be placed or bought off, precinct workers to mollify and slates to be drawn up. "If all the planning and skulduggery that goes into electioneering went into something constructive, West Virginia would be the nation's most progressive state, instead of one of the least," one member of the state House of Delegates told me.

In some counties, elections are deadly serious affairs. In others, candidates take a more lighthearted approach. Take the candidate for county sheriff who found rumors rampant that he was having sexual relations with a cow. Realizing such viciousness could destroy his political career, he scrawled "I Love You" on a sign, tied it to a spotted Holstein and led the cow through the county seat. The voters showed their appreciation by electing him sheriff, or so the story goes.

Election fraud too often is not only tolerated but anticipated. "Voters expect to get something for their vote," explained one West Virginia legislator. "They feel it's their due for belonging to the party." Through 1970, not a single person had ever been convicted of vote fraud in West Virginia, according to the Secretary of State's office, despite well-documented acts of intimidation, vote stealing and bribery. "Juries just won't convict," said one state election official. "They don't look at cheating at the polls as being bad. One state legislator I know of ran out of cash on election day a few years back, so he proceeded to buy votes with checks, but nobody would prosecute him." The same official said that during a debate over a proposed state election-reform law, one representative asked, not in jest, "What are we going to do with all the money spent on elections if this thing passes?" Another complained, "It's getting so dead people in Kentucky can't elect anyone in West Virginia anymore."

Fraud produces a wild and woolly politics of unconcern, and the region's lack of political leadership is legendary. If a candidate knows he can, and often must, buy votes to win reelection, he doesn't have to be responsive to his constituents' needs. He simply does what he feels best, or what powerful interest groups that have contributed to his campaign tell him to do. He doesn't have to see that his constituents have good roads or adequate schools, or that their tax systems are just. He doesn't have to see that they get their fair share of state or municipal services. His election doesn't depend on that sort of thing.

Too often in the past, candidates for state office have played by the same rules in dealing with the most corrupt of Appalachian counties. "They'd just come around and drop off $5,000 or $10,000 or $20,000, depending on the office, and the county machine would deliver how many votes they needed," said one legislator. "But we'd never get anything in return."

In several notable instances, the state also has gotten very little in return. The most blatant example of this latter state of affairs occurred during the administration of West Virginia Governor W. W. "Wally" Barron, who probably brought more infamy to the state than any other single politician in its history. Barron, a former Elkins, West Virginia lawyer and the son of a Presbyterian minister, served as gov-

ernor from 1961 to 1964. Since then, 21 state officials and political insiders in his administration have been indicted on
felony charges ranging from bribery and influence-peddling
payoffs to spending state money to take a Florida vacation
with a pretty blonde secretary. Eleven were convicted, although two convictions were reversed by a higher court.
Barron himself is now serving 25 years in a federal peniten-
tiary for bribing a juror.

Election antics take several forms. In many, if not most,
counties, electioneering is limited to pressuring patronage
workers, not-so-subtly threatening welfare recipients that
they better vote "right" or lose their monthly allotments or
poverty-program jobs, and hiring dozens of election workers
to do party chores at polling places and drive voters to and
from the polls. The latter practice is common to the poorer
sections of most cities, and party pros regard it as a necessary
evil to keep the wheels of democracy greased and running.
Often the payments are plain bribes based more on how
many "safe" votes an election worker can deliver from the
ranks of his friends and family than on any other service
rendered.

The formula for a winning ticket in the more corrupt
counties is more dependable, according to one state senator.
"It all depends on who controls the machines inside and the
money outside," he says. Anything from $2 to $20 buys a
vote, and sometimes votes are delivered in wholesale lots,
with a candidate or party faction paying as much as $100 to
the head of a family who controls a large block of votes. The
days of the famous moonshine vote are now largely gone, but
the half-pint "red whiskey" vote still decides some close
races. Most often it is a simple swap arrangement—a vote for
a few dollars, a half-pint or a healthy swig from the precinct
bottle, often within sight of the polling place.

The control of the election machinery inside the polling place is even more important than the payoffs outside. As one pro explained, "There's a lot of bridges some of them guys ain't doublecrossed yet." West Virginia law provides a convenient way to make sure that every vote buyer gets his money's worth. It's a provision whereby an illiterate or physically disabled voter can ask an election commissioner to go into the voting booth with him. In the most corrupt precinct "houses," or voting places, election commissioners—usually cronies and trusted allies of the entrenched political bosses—spend much of their day "helping out" illiterates and most anyone else who comes by, pulling the right levers, voting the right votes and then signaling to an outside man that the "helped out" voter has performed his civic duty and now deserves to be paid off. If a voter can't be trusted, or if he happens to be from a precinct where the commissioners are honest, or working for another party faction, he may be asked to vote before election day by absentee ballot, particularly if the circuit court clerk who collects the ballots is a trusted ally and can be counted on to record the ballot for the "right" side.

Mingo County and "The Boss"

In the fall of 1970, Noah Floyd was 53, and he didn't want to talk. Too busy, he'd say on the phone in a friendly, unassuming voice. "Try later this afternoon. Should be free then." But then he wouldn't be, and I'd try again and again, 15 times in all in 3 separate visits to Mingo County. Sometimes, he'd apologize and chat for a minute. His indictment for election fraud would come up and he'd say, "I've been in politics a good many years and certainly you make enemies . . . I feel that's the case here."

Floyd had been a reform candidate when he first won a

seat in the state House of Delegates in 1954. A devout Baptist who had grown up in the little mining town of Chattaroy, he, like dozens of ambitious young men in countless other mountain towns, chose politics as a way to get ahead. Mingo County, even in those days, had a well-established reputation as a political snake pit. The county, a land of pinched valleys and rough mountains separated from Kentucky only by the Tug River, took its name from the Mingo Indians, a band of renegades formed by outcasts from Iroquois and Shawnee tribes. The Mingos were known as cowards among other Indians and early white settlers because they never attacked an enemy village until all its men had gone hunting, leaving only women and children to defend the camp.

It was an election day shootout, a century after the Mingos had been driven from the county, that immortalized the county in American folklore. Ellison Hatfield, a Mingo County boy from Horse Pen Creek, and a number of his relatives had crossed the Tug River to vote in Blackberry Creek, Kentucky. There was the usual fighting and drinking that accompanied such affairs, and in the late afternoon Ellison found himself wrestling with a Kentuckian named Tolbert McCoy. Ellison was about to break the smaller man's neck when Tolbert's 15-year-old brother thrust a knife into Ellison's back. Wincing in pain, Ellison picked up a large rock and raised it to throw at the older McCoy. Just then someone pitched a pistol to Tolbert. He fired into Ellison's stomach. Ellison died three days later, setting the scene for the Hatfield-McCoy feud, a bloody interfamily war that eventually claimed more than 100 lives.

Warfare between the Hatfields and the McCoys died out more than 70 years ago, and the Hatfields of Mingo County have gone on to illustrious careers in law, medicine, agriculture and politics, one becoming governor of West Virginia. Another of their number has gone into the auto business with a McCoy, and their advertisements on radio station WBTH in Williamson boast, "We're not feuding, we're Fording."

Political feuding, however, is far from dead. By 1970, Noah Floyd had been in the middle of it for more than three decades. He had served eight years as a member of the state House of Delegates; eight years as a state senator; eight years as executive director of the Mingo County Taxpayers Association, an unusual lobbying group representing county industrial interests; and, most importantly, eight years as chairman of the county Democratic executive committee. It was this last post that gave him the title of "Boss" or "Kingpin" and influence right up to the governor's office in Charleston. The *Welch Daily News* in neighboring Mc-Dowell County commented on his role:

> Floyd, first of all, is the acknowledged political king over there. When he snaps his fingers, heads roll or jobs are made available, depending on the tone of the snap. Because of Floyd, Mingo County today has the worst reputation in the state for pure political shenanigans.
>
> Frankly, we think the reputation is well deserved. . . . When the Republicans got control of the statehouse, Noah Floyd didn't flinch at all. He picked up 14 former state road and liquor store employees and put them to work in the Mingo County Courthouse. The cost to Mingo taxpayers is reported to be about $69,000.

In 1968, Floyd was chosen chairman of the state Senate Elections Committee, a post that put him in an ideal position to kill any election-reform bills that might come up. His appointment was an apt one. Any politician from southern West Virginia has to learn about all there is to know about election shenanigans simply to survive. As Floyd's onetime ally and later a delegate to the state legislature, Howard Chambers, put it, "For years there's been nothing but plain crooked, stealing elections in southern West Virginia."

Election fraud may or may not have been any worse in Mingo County than in any one of half a dozen other counties in the area. But it was certainly better documented. In 1960, for instance, Mingo had 31,000 registered voters. Yet its entire population was less than 40,000, indicating that perhaps as many as 12,000 persons, or one-third of the registrants, were illegally registered. By 1963, the rolls had dropped to about 28,000 (no exact figures are available), about 10,000 below the county's population. Yet more than 17,000 of those included in the population figures were under 21 and thus ineligible to vote. Five years later a survey found that 41 percent of the voters in a general election were either bought or "encouraged" to vote for the entrenched machine. By 1970, a purge of voting rolls cut the number of eligible voters to 17,000, depriving of their "right" to vote scores of dead people and people who had moved from the county years before.

James Washington

James Washington is chairman of the Mingo County Fair Elections Committee (FEC). He is one of those surprising people you'd never expect to meet in the mountains, a product of the War on Poverty, one of its victories. In the old days, he was a coal miner; he first went into the mines when he was only 13. Today he's called a community organizer and works for the Mingo County Community Action Agency.

Washington is a short, stocky, dark-skinned Negro, full of gentleness and anger. I met him one night in mid-December in his dingy office above a drugstore in Williamson. He had spent much of the last three years fighting for clean elections, and although the politicians didn't like to admit it, his group had made the elimination of vote fraud a popular cause in the county and had spurred several election reforms.

The evidence was piled helter-skelter in the file cabinet behind him. Scores of affidavits from such people as Simon Hatfield, who charged that an election commissioner had followed him into a voting booth and changed his votes on the machine, and Mose Roberson, who claimed to have seen election workers giving bottles of whiskey to nine voters. Letters to U.S. Attorney General John Mitchell ("The whole country knows that West Virginia is notorious for unfair elections and we feel it is about time something is done about it."), and to former Governor Hughlett Smith ("The citizens of Mingo County need your protection."). Endless pamphlets ("We are dedicated to honest government."). Voter-challenger lists showing how committee members had found 79 illegal voters on the rolls in the Red Jacket precinct, 88 in the Newtown precinct, 122 in the Varney precinct and 700 in the Magnolia district.

"Elections always been crooked around here," Washington said. "People just don't get alarmed about them. Back when I started voting I was part of this stuff myself. I saw people passing money at the election door and I thought that was the way it was supposed to be—part of the routine, you know."

Washington's first real lesson in the implications of vote fraud came in 1966 when he began doing volunteer work with the local antipoverty agency, then as now one of the best in Appalachia. An old injury had driven him from the mines after 20 years underground, and he was determined "to try to get a better deal for the little fellow." But he soon found that "everywhere we turned we ran into the political bosses. It didn't matter to them what the people wanted, they had bought or stole all their votes. They knew all they had to do was throw a pot of money in come election day and they'd be reelected."

Washington soon found himself thrust into the election-committee leadership and on the antipoverty group's payroll. "First thing we needed more education, so we taught ourselves what the laws were," he said. "We spent hours studying until after awhile we found we had people knowing more about election law than the lawyers or those other fellas at the courthouse." The more the group studied, the more problems it found. It became increasingly apparent, for example, that the dominant Democratic party and the Republican party were not competing at the polls; they were trading off support. Republican election commissioners would help Democrats in the primary election, or at least not challenge what they were doing, in exchange for the Democrats' help in school-board races. "Everyone knew before that votes were bought and sold, but we really didn't know how crooked it was," Washington told me. His voice was slow and matter-of-fact.

By 1968, the Fair Elections Committee was ready for a spring offensive. One group of its members investigated padded registration rolls, challenging the eligibility of hundreds of voters. "We found one man on the books over at Dingess who had been dead 49 years," Washington recalled. "Over in Stafford one family had three daughters, all under age, voting. In some other precincts all's you had to do was pass through the county and you'd be on the books." Absentee voting was another target; still others were election commissioners and intimidation. Committee members, working with the local poverty agency, found that two-thirds of the election officers were state and county employes, many of them political appointees supervising large blocks of low-paid workers who were easy to intimidate. "It would be almost impossible to expect a fair election with these men at the polls," FEC statements drafted at the time said.

On May 14, the date of the primary election, the committee fielded the largest group of independent poll watchers —many of them students, lawyers and antipoverty workers from outside the area—in the county's history. The results were predictable. In addition to the normal vote buying and polling-place chicanery, a constable and a group of young toughs threatened to rape one committee member. A deputy sheriff threatened to shoot a camera out of the hands of another. A third poll watcher was struck by another deputy inside the county courthouse when he attempted to snap a picture of candidates mingling with voters outside the voting machines. A fourth observed three men "work on" an open voting machine in a van after polling ceased.

Washington and the FEC kept the pressure on through the fall general election. Vote buying and intimidation didn't stop. But FEC actions attracted enough attention that the FBI and the Department of Justice began belated probes, and the state legislature was on the verge of passing its first election-reform bill in decades until Noah Floyd's Senate Elections Committee killed it during the last days of the legislative session. More significantly, the Floyd machine began to crack and a factional split in it promised the first real local reform in the county in 33 years.

"Things are better now, but we still have to watch out," Washington said that December night. "The politicians still have too much control. Sometimes I think they're just waiting to get rottener.

"The main thing is you have to put some pride in people," he added after a pause. "No one can buy a vote unless it's for sale."

Mrs. Lerly Murphy

She is the proper mother: brunette, trim, tidy, younger than her years and more strong-willed than her appearance lets on. Her house on the hill above Matewan, the site of one of the bloodiest shoot-outs of the old mine-union wars, is carpeted and immaculately neat. The furnishings are early American; plain, but expensive for the area. Her husband, she says, is a railroad man, holding a good job by Appalachian standards, and he owns a television-repair shop. In 1966, he wanted to become a justice of the peace, an elective office in West Virginia. He lost in the Republican primary, partially because he wouldn't play by the accepted rules of Mingo County politics.

The election was a revelation to Mrs. Murphy. "I found it wasn't the people, but the election officers who did all the voting, not only for the poor people but the others too," she said. "I certainly didn't want my children to be involved in politics if that's the way it was going to be."

She has four children, boys aged 15 and 12, and girls aged 9 and 10. Her husband lobbied strenuously against her joining the fair-election fight; her parents "thought I was crazy." But she says she did it for them and the children. "Too many people just didn't want to step forward and do anything about it. 'I just don't want to get involved,' they'd say. Then election day would come along and the honest people would complain, 'What's the use of voting, they'll steal it anyway.' "

She gave three months of her time, four or five days a week, and also went to night meetings. "Let my house go, neglected the children—everything," she says. The experience was an education, even for someone who had spent all her life in Mingo County. At one point, Mrs. Murphy was arrested and threatened with a jail sentence. At another, a courthouse worker threatened "to pull every hair out of my head."

She talked to Social Security recipients who told her, "I have to vote for them or they'll cut off my check," and to dozens of persons "who wouldn't do anything for you unless they got $5 or $10." She spent much of her time reviewing voting rolls. She challenged the eligibility of 710 voters in all. Among them were members of a family she grew up with in north Matewan who had moved to Kentucky 30 years before, and friends who were registered in both parties or under both their maiden and married names. On election day, a deputy sheriff jostled her and her husband. Later that same day, they asked an elderly lady if she had voted. "She said, 'No, I'm waiting to see who pays the most. I need $5 or I ain't goin' to vote.'"

When it was over, she gave speeches about the election and traveled to Washington to tell of her experiences. She also went to Charleston with James Washington to receive a Rural Service Award for helping "create a better life for our citizens."

"But I really don't think they're getting any better," Mrs. Murphy said in her orderly living room. Her hands were on her crossed knees. "We worked so hard and nothing happened. We worked so hard and they didn't do anything."

Election Night

The votes from Williamson Hollow, Varney, Red Jacket, Matewan, Dingess and 31 other precincts are tallied on a huge blackboard in the basement of the county courthouse in Williamson. In tight elections, the room is full and liquor flows freely outside, on Main Street. But there was little excitement over this election. The county is almost exclusively Democratic, and the only real battles are usually in the spring primaries and the supposedly nonpartisan school-board races. This time voters would decide on a U.S. Senator, a Congressman, a state senator, two representatives to the state House of Delegates, a constable and several lesser local officeholders. But the only real interest was in a factional battle against reform Democrat Lafe Ward. Ward, a soft-spoken assistant county prosecutor, beat party kingpin Noah Floyd by 350 votes during the spring primary in a race for the state senate. Now, in the general election, Floyd forces were said to be halfheartedly working with Republicans against Ward and Howard Chambers, one of his supporters and a nominee for the House of Delegates.

Early that morning in Williamson Hollow Jack Owens had assured me no such move was afoot, that this election was strictly on the up-and-up. I told the cleaning lady at my motel what Owens had said. "You'll find a lot of that—corruption and double-talk, I mean," she said. "Used to be this town was just mean. Now it's crooked too. They're all crooked. It just depends on if he's a crook on your side or their side."

Tom Chafin was recording the early returns. He is a short man and he had to stand on a stool to reach the top of the blackboard. He is Mingo County clerk and, as such, its chief election official and keeper of its voter-registration rolls. Once he was an important cog in the Floyd machine. Now he is an insurgent, closely allied with Lafe Ward, and he has purged literally thousands of illegal voters from the registration books.

"I helped make Floyd boss," he said during an interlude.

"We thought he would do a better job than the old boss, so we busted up the old machine. That was back about 1963. By '64 we found out we didn't like what he was doing, but it was too late to do anything about it.

"What got me is he wasn't treating our people right. He got in with the Chamber of Commerce and the Mingo County Taxpayers Association [a lobbying group controlled by big utility interests]. They gave him a job with a good salary for doing nothing. What they did is buy his vote so every time something came up his vote was always bought out. He sold the ordinary fella out."

Chafin is a practical man, a politician, not an idealist. He knew how elections had been bought and sold in Mingo County for generations from firsthand experience. ("When the voting machines came in, some thought that would end all the stealing," he said. "Hell, they just made it so you could steal faster and more efficiently.") He also knew that under normal circumstances it would be nearly impossible to throw a strongman like Noah Floyd out of office. But the late 1960's were not ordinary times in Mingo County. Community-action groups sponsored by the local antipoverty program were springing up all over the county and making their weight felt in official channels. Jay Rockefeller, a young member of the state House of Delegates who later was to become secretary of state, was throwing his money around and making a name for himself by pushing for statewide election reforms. Locally, the Fair Elections Committee was exposing massive voting irregularities, and Chafin was beginning to clean up his registration rolls. (Chafin minimizes the FEC's influence. "They were trying to down me and give me a bad name," he says. "They didn't do no help at all, but they took the credit.") And the newspapers in Charleston were "giving us a lot of bad publicity."

Floyd was handling it all very poorly. His support eroded as grand juries probed his election-day activities. In the early winter of 1970, Chafin and a group of dissidents decided to challenge the boss. "It was either now or live 20 years under a dictatorship," one explained. They picked Lafe Ward, a popular former county school board member, as their candidate. He was personable, reform-minded, young and untainted.

Soon it would be official. The crowd in the basement of the Mingo County courthouse grew as returns came in one by one, hand-carried from precinct houses in Gilbert, Delbarton, Sprigg, Beech Creek, Warrencliffe and 31 other places. One election official told of instructions an old pro gave him before his first day at the polls two decades before: "Don't worry about them stuffing that ballot box," the old-timer said. "We don't count that one anyway."

The ballots were being counted this election. Tom Chafin, the county clerk, was recording them on the blackboard: Precinct No. 9, Lafe Ward, Democrat, 261, Sidney M. Copley, Republican, 67; Precinct No. 55, Ward 135, Copley, 50; Precinct No. 6, Ward 128, Copley 56. Ward failed to carry only six precincts, all traditional Democratic strongholds. One of them was Williamson Hollow, where Republican Copley outpolled Ward 147 to 65. The Democratic candidate for U.S. Congressman, James Kee, outpolled his Republican rival 194 to 12 in the same precinct. "Someone's been playing the machines on Lafe Ward," Chafin said.

But the election was decided. Ward, the insurgent reformer, had won an overwhelming victory, despite what had happened in Williamson Hollow. "You've seen a little bit of history here today," Chafin said. "Quietest election I've seen in 25 years."

Epilogue

They came one hot, sultry day in August, the poor in their denims and cotton dresses, up the clay path to the spot on the hill where the Daniel Boone Elementary School once stood. Some of them carried placards that read: "Impeach Poverty" or "Hope is the Symbol of the Poor." Others, more practical persons, carried baskets of fried chicken legs and corn bread.

It was to be a great day in the history of the poor people of Knox County, a great day in the history of the poor of Kentucky—who, everyone agreed, hadn't had many days that could even be considered good. A factory was to be dedicated, and, as the printed program said, it "will be owned and managed mainly by the poor." And so the poor came, some 1,500 strong, from Clay and Jackson and Pike and Letcher and Breathitt and Madison and a half-dozen other counties where babies sometimes go to bed hungry on cold January nights.

Knots of them gathered outside the huge cinder-block building, swapping endless tales and moistening the sun-parched ground with brown tobacco juice. Inside, scores of their brethren sat in straight-backed chairs. Up front was a rostrum decked in patriotic red, white and blue. A Republican congressman sat on it. So did a former governor, a Democrat, and a man who wanted to be governor very badly, and a stack of telegrams from senators and lesser men who said they'd like nothing better than to be present but couldn't make it.

Hollis West, the poverty general from upstate New York, had planned the occasion well. There would be banjo picking, placard waving, soul music, politicking, prayers, promises and a roomful of mountain oratory. Hands would clap in unison to the words of "The Battle Hymn of the Republic" and "My Welfare Cadillac." Sweat would roll off the foreheads of the gathered politicians and the backs of the poor, making their cotton shirts cling to the metal chairs. It was to be a grand day, the kind of day the poverty war hadn't seen in three years.

"They told us we could never do it," West said. "They said these mountain men could never build something like this, that they were too lazy or stupid. But they did it with their own hands. We showed them what could be done." West had acquired a slight twang in his three years in the mountains as executive director of the Knox County Economic Opportunity Commission, one of Appalachia's best antipoverty agencies.

On the rostrum, the dignitaries in their expensive suits waxed on and on, alternately praising and promising in the best tradition of hill-country oratory. One heralded the crude cinder-block edifice as a "cathedral to Appalachia." Someone else suggested, "We're going to move some mountains."

The politicians shed their silk jackets. The former governor reminisced how he grew up on Beech Creek in neighboring Clay County, making him a good ole mountain boy like everyone else. Everyone clapped. He didn't mention how, when his term as governor was up, he set up a law office and an insurance company to peddle influence and political favors. The man who wanted to be governor told of his equally modest beginnings on Yellow Creek in Daviess County. That's at the other end of the state and hardly anyone had ever heard of it, but everyone clapped anyway. He didn't tell how his family insurance company had written more than $40 million in state contracts while he was on the state payroll.

Congressman Tim Lee Carter was the most impressive of all. He dutifully recited how he had supported a pile of bills to help the poor folks of Knox County and the rest of his district. But that was only after he had whetted their gullets with seven minutes of good country humor: "Did you ever hear the one about the new preacher who filled the water pitcher on the pulpit with gin to spice up his first sermon? The longer he talked, the dryer his throat got. The dryer his throat got, the more he sipped. The more he sipped, the longer he talked. Each sip put more and more 'divine' inspiration into his message. After 90 minutes, he was so divinely inspired that he was saying David had not slain Goliath with a slingshot, but had taken his club and beat the living hell out of him."

The poor who made their way to the podium spoke with less polish but with deeper emotion. They talked about welfare, they talked about defeats, they talked about how the poor had to organize to let "our voices echo to the four corners of the earth," and they talked about how poor folks, if they ever wanted real power, would have to stop selling their votes even though "that $20 bill looks real good if you got five kids."

There was Verlan Golden, chairman of the Kentucky Poor People's Coalition, who wept as he dedicated the building to a fellow coalition leader who had died in an auto crash. "It's not time for promises. We've heard enough promises. We're tired of them," he said. "It's time we quit putting poor folks down as no good." There was Mrs. Ellen Wigginton, a crippled black who once presented a mule to the governor of Kentucky while he hosted the National Governors' Conference. (Governor Louie B. Nunn accepted the jackass, saying its hindquarters reminded him of "the behavior of some of those who made this presentation.") And there was Earl McIntosh, elderly and honest, a man who had seen enough of life to know that the nation's priorities were out of whack. "I got no college education. What I'm telling you here is experience," he said. "We've got a lot of good roads in Kentucky, but people can't eat roads, and when it gets cold, they can't sleep on roads. I tell you they don't mean a hill of beans. And I tell you the poor is not poor because God wanted him to be poor, he's poor because the man made him poor."

Applause for Verlan Golden. Applause for Ellen Wigginton. Applause for Earl McIntosh. Everyone agreed, even the politicians. But there was a hollow, almost mechanical, ring to the response, particularly from the poor. Their egos, their hopes had been buoyed before. They had once believed, as the former governor suggested, that the poor should organize and "make your demands known in the halls of Washington and Frankfort." They had tried that and had believed that prosperity was over the next mountain. But it hadn't come, and now some had a sinking feeling that they, or at least some of their Appalachian counterparts, had been duped. For them the War on Poverty and the Great Society were dead. The words and the applause were repeated now only because this was their last hurrah.

Six years had passed since Lyndon Johnson sat on Tom Fletcher's porch on Rockcastle Creek, five years since he pronounced, "Dole is dead." The federal government had spent over $7 billion in Appalachia during those years, enough to finance the war in Vietnam 24 weeks. Roads, courthouses, medical centers and schools had been built, doctors, lawyers and high-priced bureaucrats hired, promises made. Professors in Cambridge and writers in New York had lamented, planned and profiteered. Yet dole *wasn't* dead and it still *isn't* dead.

The Nixon administration, bogged down in a senseless war 10,000 miles away, has shown little interest in the deprivation John Kennedy found in 1960 when he tramped the coaltowns of West Virginia. Appalachia's three million poor are again forgotten. Despair still grips their isolated hollows and grimy coaltowns. The old patterns of life continue, and a new generation of welfare recipients is being born. On the eve of a new presidential campaign the people of coaltown await a new call to the nation's conscience.

This book offers no solution to the problems of Appalachia. The region has enough soothsayers and would-be experts. Neither the questions nor the answers are as easy as they were a decade ago. Nor has our ability to cope with the problems improved. The interplay of poverty, politics and welfare has frustrated our most valiant efforts. As a result, there is a disenchantment with ideas and groups that captured our imagination a short time ago when visionaries wanted to rid us of poverty once and for all. Many of us have lost faith in the poor—just as the poor have lost faith in us— because they were unwilling or unable to respond to our left-handed solutions to their problems. On top of it all, the poor acted badly. When we expected them to be docile, they were loud. When we expected them to be grateful, they were militant.

It is tempting, particularly to the outsider, to point fingers at villains in the mountains of east Kentucky and West Virginia. They make convenient scapegoats for the failures of the 1960's. And there are more than enough to go around— the corrupt union chiefs, the gutless politicians, the insensitive bureaucrats, the pushy poverty warriors, the greedy coal bosses, the power-hungry school superintendents. All have doubtlessly compounded the plight of the Appalachian highlander.

But to blindly condemn them without examining the institutions and forces that produced them is to ignore how geography hemmed the mountaineer in, how the coal and timber barons stole his natural wealth, how a nation caught up in its own quest for "progress" forgot him for almost two centuries, leaving him without democratic traditions and the skills and education necessary for our technical age. How much, for example, can we criticize a West Virginia school superintendent for not providing innovative educational leadership when he has only $385 to spend per pupil per year in his county while his average counterpart in New York State spends $1,159 per student? How much can we blame a "rich hillbilly" for wanting the kind of life our affluent society proclaims as ideal every night on network television? How much can we blame a man for taking a job as a bulldozer operator on a strip mine when it's the only employment available to him and he knows the utility companies hunger for cheap coal? How can we reasonably expect any significant change in such poverty pockets as central Appalachia without a major realignment of the attitudes and social forces that govern our whole society, and a reformation of the institutions—the schools, the courthouse gangs, the corrupt union chiefs—with which we've saddled the poor?

In a few places, such as the hill where the Boone Industrial Building stands, there is still hope. Enough hope that 45 men and women who didn't have jobs 5 years ago now pick up small paychecks every 2 weeks, thanks to a new furniture factory owned by the poor. Enough hope that the 12,000 poor people of Knox County, Kentucky, may someday have a greater voice in their own destiny.

But the question of major institutional reform persists.

So do the smaller questions that are perhaps more important to the residents of coaltown:

Will Curtis Collier, the one-legged miner from Franks Creek, get his pension?

Will the children in the one-room schoolhouse at Rye Cove ever recover from the travesty Kentucky calls education?

Will Dorothy Taylor have enough coal this winter to heat her two-room house on Powderhorn Mountain in the daytime as well as in the night?

How many pints of whiskey will it take to elect the next state senator from Mingo County?

How long will Tom Fletcher have to wait on his porch for another job, or for another President to drop by?

Will the lives of the 1,500 poor people at dedication day in Barbourville ever change? Will the politicians and the poverty workers ever make good on their promises?

"What do you think? Will things ever really change?" I asked an elderly mountaineer, his face cracked by age, as we